# Kathasatisagar

# Kathasatisagar

Prof. Raj Nehru • Dr. C.K. Gariyali

*Published by*
**PRABHAT PRAKASHAN PVT. LTD.**
4/19 Asaf Ali Road,
New Delhi-110 002 (INDIA)
e-mail: prabhatbooks@gmail.com

ISBN 978-93-94534-35-3
**KATHASATISAGAR**
*by* Prof. Raj Nehru • Dr. C.K. Gariyali



*Edition*
First, 2022

*Price*
₹ 600.00 (Rupees Six Hundred only)

*Printed at*
R-Tech Offset Printers, Delhi

In loving Memory of my father

Shri Bal Kishen Nehru

(22.03.1932–15.12.2021)

# Dedication

This book is dedicated to five-thousand-year-old Kashmiri Pandit Culture. It is dedicated to our beautiful valley of Kashmir, its creator Rishi Kashyapa. It is also dedicated to Nil Nag the Naga King, who gave us the code of conduct for living in Kashmir in harmony with nature and other originals people such as Nagas, Yaksha and Pisachas, which we still follow, even in exile. It is dedicated to our 5097 year old calendar created by Saptrishis by their meditative powers. It is equally dedicated to our Shaivite and Buddhist scholar who shared their knowledge with the world.

This book is also dedicated to the proud children of this land who carry with them the cultural heritage of Kashmir, its spiritual strength, urge for knowledge and search for truth, wherever they go. By their dispersing around the globe, the world would be a better place when they share their values with others communities and nations. For the world, each one of them will be the harbingers of human hope. They will be the torch bearers of respect for elders and teachers, Universal love and unlimited hospitality for all beings and remain steadfast on their spiritual path.

मनोहर लाल
MANOHAR LAL

मुख्यमंत्री, हरियाणा
चंडीगढ़
CHIEF MINISTER, HARYANA
CHANDIGARH

Dated: 13.12.2021

# Foreword

## Kashmiri Pandit Culture

Kashmir has been a seat of Indian Culture from times immemorial. It is one of the earliest kingdoms existing even before the times of Mahabharata. Sri Krishna visited Kashmir and coronated Yashomati, the Queen of Kashmir.

Pandavas visited Kashmir during their *agyatvas*. There is evidence in Buddhist texts that Gautama Buddha visited Kashmir.

The fourth and the last Buddhist Council was held at Harvan in Kashmir in the first century AD under the patronage of Emperor Kanishka. Hieun Tsang (Xuanzang), the Chinese scholar who visited Kashmir in the seventh century, mentions that more than 500 Buddhist and Hindu scholars participated in the Council which was presided over by a Kashmiri Vasu Mitra. Nagarjuna, the great Bodhisattva, lived and worked in Harvan for many years. He also mentions about the exceptional calibre of Kashmiri and as per the directions of his host King Durlabh Vardhan, twenty Kashmiri Pandit scholars helped him in translating Buddhist Texts in Sanskrit and Pali into Chinese.

Kashmir played a great role in spreading Buddhism in Central Asia, Afghanistan, China, Sumatra, Japan and Korea. More scholars from Kashmir went to preach the message of Buddha than from the rest of India. This included Kumarajiva who translated the famous Lotus Sutra of Buddha from Sanskrit to Chinese and Prince Gūnavarma of Kashmir who abdicated his throne to become a monk.

Of the twenty-four treatises in Sanskrit, twenty-two were composed in Kashmir and only two in the rest of ancient India. According to the local legend great dramatist, Kalidas was born in Kashmir and due to the oppressive rule of King Ananda left Kashmir and moved to other parts of India, spending a long time in Ujjain. Many of his works especially 'Meghdoot' and 'Kumarsambhava' are inspired by the landscape and pristine imagery of Kashmir. It is said that he came back to Kashmir towards the end of his life and settled there when peace prevailed.

Though, according to 'Natyashastra' of Bharata Muni, dance is universally performed in India and is the basis of classical dance forms, the main treatise on dance was written by Abhinava Gupta, a scholar from Kashmir. Not only that the oldest mention of dance being performed according to Bharat Muni's 'Natyashastra' comes from the Sun Temple Martand, where as early as in the sixth-century, temple dancers danced when the King visited the temple.

Sangeet Ratnakar is the basis of classical Indian Music- both Hindustani and Carnatic. The author of 'Sangeet Ratnakar' Sarang Dev's family moved from Kashmir to Deccan during the period of oppressive rule in Kashmir.

Kashmir is the only place where the history of 5000 years is available in written records such as 'Nilmat Puram' and 'Rajatarangini' written by great historian Kalhana. Kashmiri scholars have also made a tremendous contribution to folklore by producing 'Brihat Katha' in the Paishachi language and later readopting it in Sanskrit as 'Katha Saritsagar'. The Katha Saritsagar, an ocean of tales, is the fountainhead from where all the folk tales in India and outside India have originated, including the famous Vikram and Betal stories.

Kashmir boasted of not one but three Universities that functioned on the lines of Nalanda and Taxila Universities. The University of Harvan was a great centre of Buddhist learning. The University at Vijay Vihar was a great centre of literature, poetry, grammar, Hindu and Buddhist philosophy, astrology, astronomy, mathematics, painting, sculpture, musicology and more. The University of Sharada Peeth which was visited by both Adi Shankara as well as Ramanuja was the highest centre of spiritual learning, Shaivism, Advaita etc. Unfortunately, all these were destroyed along with their precious manuscripts and libraries in the same way as the universities of Nalanda and Taxila.

The setback to the fountainhead of knowledge, the land of Kashmir, from 14th century has proved fatal to knowledge growth in Kashmir and the rest of India. The advent of foreign rule and policies of intolerance saw a rapid decline of intellectual pursuits in Kashmir.

We do not see even one outstanding work from Kashmir after the 14th century. Not even in Persian or Urdu, the new languages forced into the State. This has caused the demise of the intellect not only in Kashmir but India.

I am very happy to write the foreword for this book Kathasatisagar by our own scholar from Haryana, Shri Raj Nehru, the Vice-Chancellor of Shri Vishwakarma Skill University and Dr. Chander Kanta Gariyali a retired IAS officer and former Secretary to the Governor of Tamil Nadu.

While reading the book, I was most impressed by the fact that women held a very high status in Kashmiri society. There have been very few saint poets in India barring Mira Bai in North and Andal and Avvayar in South. It was a matter of pleasure for me to know that Kashmir produced two outstanding women saint poets, Lal Ded and Rupa Bhawani who uttered immortal golden verses or *vakhs*.

I truly feel that this book is not only about the cultural heritage of Kashmir but the cultural heritage of India of which we all can be proud. This book should be in all libraries and in schools and colleges in India.

**(Manohar Lal)**
Chief Minister, Haryana

# Preface

While I was writing my book 'Kashmir—The Land of Kashyapa: The Saga of Kashmiri Pandits', I requested Raj Nehru to write a foreword for my book. I found him to be extremely proud of being a Kashmiri Pandit. At that time, he informed me that he has been gathering many interesting aspects about the culture of the Kashmiri Pandits and has been writing small stories around them as a hobby. I found that both of us were passionate about similar things and cherished our heritage which we do not want to be forgotten. We decided to collaborate to write a book together. This work is the result of our collaboration. It is our tribute to Kashmir, to its loving people, to its ancient heritage and to the great contribution it has made to the society within and outside India.

Through this work, we celebrate our great books like *Nilamata Purana*, *Brihatkatha*, *Kathasaritsagar* and *Rajatarangini*. We celebrate our holy places, our unique customs and festivals.

The book looks at our sacred geographies such as our holy river *Vitasta*, our sacred mountain *Harmukh*, our most revered *Shankaracharya* hills and our numerous scared springs and lakes.

It mentions the glories of our great centres of learning and universities such as the Sharada Peeth, Vijay Vihar and Harwan.

It talks about the Hindu and Buddhist traditions of Kashmir and pays tribute to some of the scholars, sages and saints belonging to these traditions.

The ultimate objective of this book is to share the pride of Kashmiri Culture with our younger generation so that they know who they are and work to take these traditions forward.

Buddh Purnima
16th May, 2022

**—Dr. C.K. Gariyali,** IAS (Retd.)

# Message

Kashmiri Pandits, post their forced exodus, have witnessed a large scale forward migration of compulsion of their community across the nation and also outside the country. The instinct of surviving in difficult situations that this community has learnt in the last 700 years has made them to steer through this seventh exodus with a grace. While education continues to be their key strength, many community members have pursued higher studies, jobs, business, livelihood and other fields by further migrating to other regions inside or outside India. While to a large extent, this migration has significantly eroded their economic, social and political status, many have still managed and have been perhaps fortunate to achieve success through their individual leadership qualities.

However, the exodus has miserably weakened the cultural understanding amongst the community youngsters to a large extent not because they are not interested but due to availability of a poor ecosystem to nurture and support their culture, rituals and practices, that has been lost due to the forced exodus and forward migration. Almost two generations have now lost connect with their roots resulting in a poor understanding of their set of a distinctive spiritual, intellectual, emotional, religious & ethnic features including the ways of living together, values, traditions, beliefs and lifestyle. These aspects have provided a sense of identity, belongingness and safety to the whole community for ages. Unfortunately, this exodus has not only deprived the whole community of their sense of identity, safety and dignity but also their human rights as a community as well. As per UNESCO, cultural rights of anyone, including the ethnic communities is an integral part of their human rights. While the ethnic cleansing was one of the gravest crimes committed on this minority ethnic community, there is also an issue of a serious human right violation that they have been continuously subjected to, unabated.

The UNESCO Declaration talks about culture and identity as being part of our human rights and fundamental parts of development, in a national sense. Cultural rights are an integral part of human rights which are universal, indivisible, and interdependent.

This book is an attempt to put together a small glimpse of a large culture and heritage that is thousands of years old with a distinctive identity. My interactions with my father were an inspiration to write and compile some of them in an easier to understand manner for our younger generation that can be a facilitative tool in growing, developing and refining them as community members. The other objective is also to address the issue of cultural assimilation that may be silently happening due to a massive geographical dispersion of our community members into other dominant cultural groups. This dispersion may be resulting into the loss of some or virtually all of the age old cultural behaviours, practices, beliefs and values amongst our young community members.

The attempt of this book is to provide insights and visibility to some of our cultural and ethnic practices that can inspire our youths and rekindle the desire for our rich heritage, language and values and also inspire their progeny to follow the same.

The book has been named as "Kathasatisagar", given that

all the stories pertain to the land of Sati and only a few stories could be picked from the ocean of stories.

I thank my co author Dr. C.K. Gariyali, IAS for her cooperation and support while writing and compiling this book.

**—Raj Nehru**
Vice Chancellor-SVSU

# Acknowledgment

We acknowledge using the writings from books and articles of following authors who inspired us to produce this volume.

Dr. Mark Dyczkowski
David Peter Lawrence
Shri Jawahar Lal Ganhar
Dr. Krishna Raina
Shri Pradeep Khali
Shri T.N. Dhar
Shri S.N. Fotedar
Shri Narender Sehgal
Dr. C.L. Raina
Shri Dileep Langoo
Dr. Jai Kishan Sharma
Omanand Koul - Massachusetts
Shri M.L. Bhat
Dr. A.N. Raina
Mrs. Aparna Dhar
Shri Upendra Ambardar
Shri Chander Mohan Bhat
Dr. Ved Kumari Ghai
Mr. Zahid G. Muhammad
Shri Shashi Shekhar Toshkhani

Swami Lakshmanjoo
Shri K.N. Pandita
Dr. Satish Ganjoo
Dr. Santosh Kaul
Shri C.L. Gadoo
Shri R.K. Taimiri
Shri Suraj Tickoo
Swami Bodasarananda
Prof. R.K. Pandit
Shri J.N. Bhat
Shri T.N. Dhar
Shri S N Fotedar
Shri P.N. Gnhar
Shri Dileep Langoo
Shri Pyare Lal Raina
Shri Narender Sehgal
Shri Jai Kishore Pandit
Neerja Mattoo
Zahid G. Muhammad
Noble Timothy Myers
Martin Iversen
Shernaz Wades
Shri Brij B. Kachroo
Shri M.L. Bhat
Dr. A.N. Raina
Mrs. Aparna Dhar
Shri Chander Mohan
Shri O.N. Koul
Arun Jallalı
Altaf-ur Rehman

We have also obtained extensive help from
Nilmat Puran
Rajtarangini
Vanamali Ashram writings
Koshur Samachar

Barishta-i-Shahi

Tohfatu'l-Ahbab

Kashmiri Pandit website such as Kashmiri Pandit Network, Habba Kadal, Shehjar, Iqwat, Saints of Kashmir and others.

We are grateful to Senior artists Shri Ravi Dhar, for permitting us to use his images.

We have also used images of Ratan Parimoo, Shivani Kaul Bhat, Dmple Kaul, Savi Bhat and from IQWAT collection.

# Contents

# Part-1

# History, Culture and Ancient Kashmir

# Nilamata Purana

*Nilamata Purana* is an ancient text dating back to the 6th century or before.

It is also known as *Kasmira Mahatmya.* When it was written, Kashmir included parts of North India, Pakistan, Afghanistan, Khorasan, and Tajikistan. Ancient historian Kalhana mentions *Nilamata Purana* as one of the important sources of the ancient history of *Kasmira.*

According to George Buhler, who is credited with saving the manuscript, *Nilamata Purana* is an important source of the cultural and political life of ancient Kashmir. In his report, he says, "Its great value lies therein that it is a real mine of information regarding the sacred places of Kashmir and their legends which are required to explain *Rajatarangini* and that it shows how Kalhana has used his sources."

*Nilamata Purana,* besides the account of sacred places, also gives a lot of information about the Kashmiri way of living. The picture of ancient *'Kasmira'* presented by its study is significant and supplementary to that of the *Rajatarangini.* While the *Rajatarangini* acquaints us with kings, queens and ministers of *'Kasmira'*, the *Nilamata Purana* generally speaks of common men in their homes, streets, gardens and temples. It talks about their food and drinks they consumed, the amusements they resorted to, their secular and spiritual thinking and the rites and ceremonies they performed throughout the year.

Below are given some interesting excerpts from the *Nilamat Purana*.

## Importance of Kashmir

Vaisampayana points out the importance of Kashmir by referring to its numerous charms and its identification with Goddess Uma. He points out further that the valley was originally a lake known as Satisaras. This leads to the question about the origin of 'Kashmir' to which Vaisampayana replies by relating a dialogue held previously between Gonanda and the sage Brihadashwa.

Brihadashwa gives, at first, the account of the divisions of time, the destruction of the world at the end of *manvantara,* the preservation of Manu and the seeds in a ship, the birth of the land and the lake, of Sati, the origin of various tribes from Kashyapa and Vishnu's allotment of Satisaras to the Nagas. Then follows the story of the demon Jalodbhava born in the waters and reared by the Nagas.

Having obtained boons from Brahma, the demons began to destroy the descendants of Manu dwelling in the lands of Darvabhisara, Gandbars Jubundura, the Sakas, the Khasas etc. Seeing this devastation, Nila, the king of the Nagas approached his father Kashyapa and prayed to him to intercede with the gods to punish the evil-doer and to save the innocent victims. He requested the gods, Brahma, Vishnu and Shiva to do the needful. Vishnu followed by Brahma, Shiva and various other deities proceeded to Naubandhana to punish the demon. The demon was imperishable in the waters; so Vishnu asked Ananta to make an outlet for the waters by breaking forth the mountain-barriers. He did accordingly. Vishnu then cut off the demon's head with his disc. With the dry land now being available in the valley, Kashyapa expressed the desire that it should be inhabited by the Nagas as well as by the descendants of Manu.

The Nagas, however, flatly refused to have the Manavas (descendants of Manu) as their co-habitants. Filled with rage, Kashyapa cursed them to live with the Pisachas. At the request of Nila, the curse was modified to the extent that the Pisachas would go every year for six months to the sea of sand and the Manavas would live in the land jointly with the Nagas during that period. Vishnu further assured the Nagas that the occupation of Kasmira valley by the Pisachas would last for only four ages.

After the passing away of the four ages, the Manavas, as usual, had gone out for six months. An old Brahmana, Candradeva did not accompany them. Troubled by the Pisachas, he approached the Naga King Nila and begged of him to ordain that 'Kasmira' might henceforth be inhabited by the Manavas without the fear of emigration. Nila complied with this request on the condition that the Manavas should follow his instructions revealed to him by Keshava. Candradeva lived for six months in the palace of Nila and was initiated into the mysteries of rites or ceremonies prescribed by Nila. In Chaitra, when the emigrant Manavas came back to Kashmir, he related the whole incident to Virodaya - King of Manavas, who agreed to the conditions.

The lengthy dialogue held between Nila and Candradeva describes sixty-five rites, ceremonies and festivals, many of which are similar to those mentioned in other Puranaic works and observed in many parts of India, while a few are peculiar to Kasmira only. At Janamejaya's enquiry as to what Gonanda had asked after listening to the teachings, another dialogue between Gonanda and Brihadashwa follows. Gonanda expresses his desire to know the names of the principal Nagas dwelling in Kasmira and Brihadashwa enumerates not fewer than six hundred Nagas. He expresses his inability to enumerate all the Nagas, as their number was too great. He further refers to four Nagas, the guardians of directions and relates the story of the Naga Sadangula and the Naga Mahapadma.

## Sacred Places

There is another dialogue between Gonanda and Brihadashwa referring to various sacred places dedicated to

Shiva. Two names of Shiva, Bhuteshvara and Kapalesvara are mentioned. It is followed by the mention of the sacred places dedicated to Vishnu and other *tirthas* situated in the valley.

Vaisampayana, Ved Vyasa's pupil says that high-souled venerable Vyasa did not include *Nilamata Purana* in the most interesting *Mahabharata* lest that should become too exhaustive with the inclusion of treatises which were not universally relevant.

## Why Kashmir did not participate in the war of Mahabharata

According to *Nilamata Purana*, Kashmir did not participate in the war of Mahabharata along with other kingdoms of India though it was a very important kingdom. It is explained in the dialogue between Janamejeya and Vaisampayana the pupil of Ved Vyasa as follows:

The King of Kashmir Gonanda was invited by his relative Jarasandha to join him in the war against the Yadavas. Gonanda joined the war and was killed by Krishna's brother Balarama during the battle. Gonanda's son Damodara wanted to avenge his father's death. When Lord Krishna was in Gandhara attending a *svayamvara* ceremony, he decided to go to Gandhara to kill Krishna but instead, Krishna killed him. Keeping in view the sacred special status of Kashmir and the womenfolk of the region, Krishna coronated Damodara's pregnant widow Yashomati, as the ruler of Kashmir. Thus Yashomati became the first woman ruler of Kashmir.

After some years, when the Mahabharata war took place, her son was still a minor. Yashomati chose not to participate in the war of Mahabharata from either side and remained neutral and saved her region from ruin caused by the war in the rest of India.

□

# Rajatarangini

According to Encyclopedia Britannica, *Rajatarangini* meaning the River of Kings is a historical chronicle of early India written in Sanskrit verse by the Kashmiri Brahmin Kalhana in 1148 AD that is justifiably considered to be the best and most authentic work of its kind. It covers the entire span of 5000 years of the history of the Kashmir region from the earliest times to the date of its composition. It is written in 7826 verses and divided into eight books.

According to a Sanskrit scholar from Varanasi, Shri Rajneesh Shukla, *Rajatarangini* is a historical chronicle of early India, written in Sanskrit verse by the Kashmiri Brahmin Kalhana in 1148, and is justifiably considered to be the best and most authentic work of its kind. It covers the entire span of history in the Kashmir region from the earliest times to the date of its composition. Kalhana is regarded as Kashmir's first historian. Like the *Shahnameh* is to Persia, the *Rajatarangini* is to Kashmir.

Kalhana is a renowned name in the world of history, not just because of his work on Kashmir, but also because of what he wrote about the process of historiography and introduces the qualities of a good historian. He argues why his *Rajatarangini* is better than the previous texts. Among his sources were a variety of epigraphic sources relating to royal eulogies, construction of temples, and land grants, coins, monumental remains, family records, local traditions.

Kalhana was able to write an unbiased and clear historical writing without any pressure from the kings because he didn't get patronage from any king of his time. His writing was devoid of rhetoric and praise, which was visible in the works of other writers under the patronage of the kings. Kalhana says, "A good history has the power to take the person into the past and explore in a way like an eye witness. That history involves a superior kind of creativity which retains its relevance even after many centuries. That historian should be appreciated who honestly judges the past incidents; unaffected by his personal likes & dislikes."

Kalhana delved deep into such works as the *Harsacarita* and the *Brihat-Samhita* epics and used with commendable familiarity the local *rajakathas* (royal chronicles) and previous works on Kashmir as *Nripavali* by Kshemendra, *Parthivavali* by Helaraja, and *Nilamata Purana*.

## Translations and Adaptations

*Rajatarangini* has always attracted people for being a unique document and has been translated into many languages. The first translation was commissioned in Persian by Sultan Zain-ul-Abidin who ruled Kashmir in the 15th century.

Horace Hayman Wilson partially translated and wrote an essay based on it titled, 'The Hindu History of Kashmir' which was published in the Asiatic Researches Volume 15.

It was translated as the 'Kings of Kashmira' by Jogesh Chandra Dutt in 1879.

Shri Ranjit Sitaram Pandit, husband of Vijay Lakshmi Pandit translated it into English as 'The Saga of the Kings of Kashmir' in 1935.

Mark Aurel Stein translated it as Kalhana's *Rajatarangini*.

It has been translated into Hindi by several scholars including Ramtej Shastri Pandey, by Vishwa Bandhu, Pandit Gopi Krishna Shastri.

The French translation was done by M. Anthony Troyer and its Urdu translation was done by Pandit Thakar Acharchand Shahpuriah and the Telugu translation was done by Renduchintala Lakshmi Narasimha Sastry.

The stories from *Rajatarangini* were also adapted by many authors such as 'Tales from The Rajatarangini' by S.L. Sadhu in 1967.

Stories from Rajatarangini -Tales from Kashmir, Amar Chitra Katha also published Chandrapeeda and other tales of Kashmir in 1984 and The Legend of Lalitaditya: Retold from Kalhana's Rajatarangini. A TV serial named Meeras was relayed in 1986 in Doordarshan Srinagar.

□

# Kathasaritsagara

One would have heard of the *Panchtantra* and *Jataka* tales, but how many have heard about the *Kathasaritsagara*, the gift of Kashmir in the form of the ocean of stories?

The *Kathasaritsagara* contains stories within a story. The original stories were written in an older version called 'Brihatkathamanjari' by Gunadhya of Kashmir in the Paisachi language. It was the language spoken by the Paisachi tribe, one of the ancient tribes who lived in Kashmir along with Nagas and Yakshas. The original work is not available but many later adaptations exist as *Brihatkathamanjari* by Kshemdendra, *Kathasaritsagara* by Somadeva and *Brihatshlokasamgraha* by Budhasvamin. The most popular of these versions is *Kathasaritsagara*.

It was written by Somadeva, son of Rama, a Shaivite Brahmin of Kashmir around 1063–81 CE.

Somadeva introduces his work as a sincere translation of a much larger earlier work *Brihatkathamanjari* of Gunadhya. Somadeva was a court poet of King Ananta. He wrote *Kathasaritsagara* to amuse Queen Suryavati, wife of King Ananta and her sons Prince Kalasa and Prince Harsha. Somadeva's style is simple and captivating. He skillfully and elegantly describes the real-life characters which keep readers focused on the stories.

It is the largest existing collection of Indian tales. The

main character is Naravahanadatta, son of Legendary King Udayana of Kosambi. As many as 350 stories are built around the central narrative of the life of Naravahanadatta, his adventures, his romances with women of extraordinary beauty, his marriages to various earthly as well as celestial damsels and the numerous wars he won. Finally, he was elevated to the rank of King of Vidyadharas, a class of heavenly spirits.

It is a large work containing 18 books, 124 Chapters, 22,000 *Shlokas* and 66,000 lines. In comparison, Milton's Paradise Lost contains only 10,565 lines. The original legendary *Brihatkathamanjari* is supposed to have contained 7 lakh *shlokas.*

Like the *Panchatantra* stories, the stories from Kathasaritsagara travelled to different parts of the world and were even absorbed in local folklore.

A part of the Kathasaritsagara became well-known as *Vetala Panchavimshati, (Betal Pachisi)* more popularly known as *Vikram-Betal* stories, where the *betal* (vampire) tells King Vikramaditya a new story every time. We have read these stories in *Chandamama* magazine in our childhood but we never realised that they were from Kashmir.

## Times of Somdeva

Unfortunately, by the time Somadeva completed his work, the princes grew up. Kalasa was a worthless degenerate prince while Harsha was capable and brilliant but ruthless. Harsha usurped the throne from his father and kept him under arrest. These events lead King Ananta to finally commit suicide and Queen Suryavati becoming a sati by self-immolating herself on the funeral pyre of the king, making it a dark and tragic period in the history of Kashmir.

## A Story from Kathasaritsagara

We present below a story from the collection translated by Shri Satya Chetan.

## Integrity–A lesson from Kathasaritsagara

King Yashodhana was an ideal king, whose life illustrates the kind of commitment and loyalty a leader among men commands by virtue of his integrity. The name Yashodhana means 'rich in fame'. He was the ruler of the kingdom of Kanakapura, the 'City of Gold', situated on the banks of the river Ganges. He was famous all over the world for his virtues.

There was a rich merchant in his city, who had an indescribably beautiful daughter Unmandini. By the time she reached the age nubile, she had grown into such rare beauty that could not be found in the entire three worlds. Such was Unmadini's beauty that just by one look at her, a man lost his head – and that is what her name meant, the one who turned men mad.

The merchant now felt it was his duty as a citizen to offer her to his king before he offered her to anyone else in marriage since by tradition, every rare jewel found in the kingdom belonged to the king. And of course, his daughter was an unsurpassed jewel. The merchant, therefore, went to the court and requested the king to accept his daughter as his wife, describing her as a precious beauty.

The king certainly was not averse to the idea. However, he had to make sure that the girl possessed the *lakshanas*–auspicious signs and marks, required in a royal bride and did not have any defects in her, which would disqualify her from being a queen. He sent a few Brahmins to the merchant's house as was the custom of the day. The Brahmins took one look at the girl and instantly lost their head – indeed, she was so maddeningly beautiful. Recovering, they consulted among themselves. There was not a doubt the girl was fit for the king in every way but her beauty! If the king wedded her, he would lose his head over her in no time and then he would lose all interest in ruling the kingdom; instead would spend all his days and nights in the rapture of worshipping her beauty. No, they couldn't afford that. They needed a king who would rule, not one lost in mad love to the beauty of a woman.

The Brahmins went back and told the king that she was unfit for his *antahpura*–her *lakshanas* were inauspicious. The king rejected her and the merchant, with the king's consent, gave her in marriage to the king's commander-in-chief Shaktidhara.

Shaktidhara loved her and they had a happy married life. Unmandini never forgot her humiliation, though. She had been rejected by the king on the grounds that her *lakshanas* were inauspicious–and she knew she had no inauspicious *lakshanas* in her and she was, beyond a doubt, a woman of unsurpassed beauty.

□

# Part-2

# Buddhism in Kashmir

# Buddhist Heritage of Kashmir

As young children, during a *havan,* we heard Guruji propitiating three Buddhist divines, *triratanas* including Buddha, Dharma and Sangha along with the Vedic and Hindu gods and goddesses. This ritual is a vestige of our Buddhist past and has been preserved by the Kashmiri Pandits due to their reverence for Buddha.

Not only that, our ancestors fasted on the day of Buddha *Purnima,* the day Buddha was born, attained enlightenment as well as Nirvana. For ancient Kashmiris, *Vaishakha Purnima* was a day of great celebration.

## Nilamata Purana on Vaishakha Purnima or Buddha Purnima

*Nilamata Purana* described the celebration of Vaisakha Purnimain Kashmir which was celebrated with great pomp. It says Buddhist monasteries, chaityas, stupas and the viharas' were decorated with flowers and paintings. Lord Buddha's statues were adorned with *Aushadhis and Ratans.*

This day was sacred to the Kashmiri Pandits and they initiated new ventures on Buddha Purnima. The great Kashmiri scholar Kshemendra (10-11th AD) commenced writing his famous treatise 'Avdhankalaplataon' on this auspicious day. The written sources show that this tradition continued till the Islamic period.

## Reference to Buddha's visit to Kashmir

Generally, it is believed that Emperor Ashoka was responsible for introducing Buddhism in Kashmir. However, our ancestors knew of Buddha even before Ashoka. The Chinese sources say that Buddhism reached Kashmir just within 50 years of the *Mahaparinirvana* of *Tathagata*.

Sir Charles Elliot, in his book, 'Hinduism and Buddhism' mentions Buddha's visit to Kashmir:

"For some two centuries after Gautama's death, we have little information as to the geographical extension of his doctrine, but some of the Sanskrit versions of the *Vinaya* text represent Buddha visiting Mathura, North-West India and Kashmir."

## Participation of Kashmiri Scholars in Third Buddhist Council

Another text, *Divyavadana* says that several scholars from Kashmir were invited by Ashoka to Patliputra to attend the Third Buddhist council held in 247 BC, which indicates that Buddhism already existed in Kashmir before the reign of Ashoka. He might have strengthened it further.

## Contribution of Majjhantika

According to the Buddhist tradition Majjhantika (Manikantaka), a disciple of Ananda from Varanasi brought the message of Buddha to Kashmir. Sri Lankan scriptures also mention that after the conclusion of the Third Buddhist Council in Patliputra, Ashoka sent missionaries across countries to spread Buddhism. Majjhantika was sent to Kashmir and Gandhara (present-day Afghanistan). The story of Majjhantika is also narrated in Buddhist scriptures Ashokavadana and Avadnkalpala. He also was associated with the introduction of saffron in Kashmir.

## Saffron Cultivation in Valley–Gift of Buddhist Monks

As teenagers, we have visited 'Pampar' ancient 'Padam Pur' (the city of Lotus) in Kashmir where the Saint Poetess Lal

Ded, also known as Padmavati lived and created a lotus pond. We were told that the pond existed till recent times.

*The Illustration of Fourth Buddhist Council*

Pampore, also known as Pampar is also the place where the renowned and highly prized saffron is grown. Ancient sources say that saffron cultivation was brought to Kashmir by Buddhist monks. As per the Chinese sources, it was Majjhantika, the early preacher of Buddhism in Kashmir, who introduced the farming and cultivation of saffron in the valley. These sources also say that Buddhist monks used to dye their robes orange with this divine spice. Later sources say that two Sufis brought saffron cultivation from Iran in the 12th century which is also possible but it is amply evident that they did not introduce saffron in Kashmir.

The old scriptures show that saffron cultivation was known in Kashmir for over 2,000 years and saffron was used in rituals such as putting a *Tilak* on the forehead and for worship, medicinal and flavouring purposes in Kashmir and the rest of the country from ancient times. Thus, it is quite likely that saffron is indeed a gift of the early Buddhist monks to Kashmir.

□

# Harwan Monastery and University

The excavations at Harwan reveal archaeological remains dating from the 1st to 6th century CE. During this period, numerous Buddhist monasteries dotted Kashmir but those at Harwan and Ushkur in Baramulla were most prominent. Even the present 'Pari Mahal' near the Chashme-Shahi Garden was the site of an important Monastery.

We have seen many exquisite terracotta tiles from the Harwan excavations in Shri Pratap Singh Museum in Jammu. According to Prashant Mathawan, some of these tiles date back to the 4th Century AD. He also says that the upper tier of the excavation site contained a temple-like round structure and a courtyard that was once covered with similar terracotta tiles. Behind this upper tier, are the remains of many more structures that are still to be excavated. It appears that the Buddhist University and settlement once covered the entire hillside.

## Fourth Buddhist Council at Harwan

Kashmir had the honour of hosting the Fourth and the last Buddhist Council at Harwan University. Nagarjuna, the great Buddhist scholar lived and worked at Harwan during the reign of Kanishka. When Kanishka held the Fourth Buddhist Council under his patronage in the 1st century AD, he appointed Nagarjuna to guide the council. Vasu Gupta, a learned Kashmir

Brahmin presided over the council with Ashvagosha as his deputy.

Following the Fourth Buddhist council, a large number of Kashmiri intellectuals took to missionary work and hundreds of the wisest sons of Kashmir carried the torch of Indian civilisation, culture and Buddhism to other parts of the world. They served as harbingers of a new age of emancipation. The maximum number of Buddhist missionaries who went to Tibet, China, Afghanistan, Korea, Java, Sumatra, Central Asia, Japan and other places were Kashmiri scholars and philosophers. Dr. P.C. Bagchi, a noted Indologist, in his book 'India and China' writes:

Kashmir takes the leading part in the transmission of Buddhist thought and traditions directly to Tibet and China. The number of Buddhist scholars who went to China from Kashmir alone is larger than those who went from the rest of India. Kashmir was the most flourishing centre of Buddhist learning in this period. It was the centre of the most powerful Buddhist sect of Northern India, known as *'Sarvastivada'.* Some of the most important Buddhist missionaries from Kashmir were Kumarajiva, Vimalaksha, Sanghbuti, Gautam, Sangha, Buddviyasa, Buddhijiva, Gunavarman, Dharamputra, Shyama Bhata and Yasa.

Padma Bhushan Dr. Lokesh Chandra, an eminent scholar and author of *India's Contribution to World Thought and Culture* has described the richness and vastness of the Kashmiri Pandit Culture and their contribution to the transformation of Indian and International thought. He seemed to have come across an inscription that reveals the following:

1. The great temples of Khajuraho were built in accordance with the guidelines of temple architecture laid down by the Kashmiri Pandits in their Tantra Shastras.
2. Kashghar was the place where the Kashmiri Pandits taught the Vedas due to which the place has acquired the name 'Kashi-Ghar'. When the scholars from

Kashghar wanted to study Vedantas and other higher subjects, they came to Kashmir for further studies.

3. Kashmiri Pandits went to Central Asia, Tibet, China, Korea, Japan and the Philippines for the dissemination of culture, art and philosophy.
4. The Siddham calligraphy was a gift of the Kashmiri Pandits to Japan.
   Japan has a tradition of writing Sanskrit shlokas in Siddham. It is a major art in Japan which was taught to them by two great Kashmiri Pandit scholars, Prajna and Munishri.
5. Several Kashmiri scholars went to Korea where Tyaghabadra and his disciples were responsible for choosing the city of Seoul, the present capital of South Korea.

□

# Buddhist Missionaries from Kashmir

As already mentioned, the largest number of Buddhist missionaries went to preach outside India from Kashmir. Here we would like to mention some of the outstanding scholars. According to Neha Munshi, a Canadian researcher, Dharmaraksa, a *Mahayana* monk from Kashmir, went to the kingdom of Kucha and worked in the court of a king at Gansu in China. Buddhayasa was another Kashmiri Brahmin who went to Central Asia and worked with a young Buddhist monk, Kumarajiva in Kucha.

## Kumarajiva

The great Buddhist scholar Kumarajiva came to Kashmir, all the way from Khotan (Kucha), the present Badakhshan, to study Sanskrit, Ayurveda and Astrology with Kashmiri scholars. He later went to China to spread the message of Mahayana Buddhism. Kumarajiva was the son of Kumarayana, a Kashmiri Brahmin, a nobleman and a scholar, who left Kashmir for Central Asia and worked as a *Purohita,* a royal priest, in the court of King Jiva of Kucha. He eventually married the Kucha princess Jivaka. Kumarajiva was born to them, probably in 334 AD.

Kumarajiva's mother Jivaka took holy vows to become a nun when Kumarajiva was only seven and joined the Tsio-li nunnery, north of Kucha. At the age of seven, Kumarajiva had already by-hearted several sutras and texts. At Tsio-li, he studied *Abhidharma* for two years. At the age of nine, his mother brought him to Kashmir to be educated under Kashmiri Scholar Bandhudatta with whom he studied *Dirgha Agama, Madhyama Agama* and the *Ksudraka.*

He was an exponent of Nagarjuna's Madhyamika School of Mahayana Buddhism. He also spread Satyashidi and Nirvana forms of Buddhism in China.

When he was just 20, King Po-Shun requested Kumarajiva to return to Kucha to instruct his daughter A-kie-ye-mo-ti, who had become a nun. He lived there in a new monastery built by king Po-Shun. Kumarajiva invited Kashmiri scholar and his mentor Vimalaksa to Kucha and studied Sarvastivadin Vinaya Pitaka under him.

Later, he went to Kashgar while his mother Jivaka remained in Kashmir. In Kashgar, he ordained two princes. There he continued his studies of *Abhidharma Pitaka,* four Vedas, five sciences, sacred Hindu texts, astronomy and many agamas under another Kashmiri Scholar Buddhayasa.

Kumarajiva was well-versed in several languages including Sanskrit. His greatest contribution has been the translation of the *Lotus Sutra* from Sanskrit to Chinese in the fourth century AD. The Lotus Sutra in Japan today is considered to be the greatest and most popular Sutras of Buddhism.

He has also translated the *Diamond Sutra, Amitabha Sutra, Vimalakirti Nirdesa Sutra* to name a few.

He later went to China to spread the message of Mahayana Buddhism. The Chinese emperor conferred upon him the title of *Tugsheo* (though young in years but ripe in wisdom) for his outstanding contribution in popularising Buddhism. He was hailed by emperor Yao Xing as a great master and enjoyed a very high status in the Buddhist court. The emperor looked upon him as his teacher. He taught many students and created a huge translation bureau where many scholars worked on translating Sanskrit texts into Chinese.

The emperor was highly influenced by his teachings of Ahimsa–non-violence and avoided wars and raids which may lead to many deaths. He also became gentler with his opponents. It is said that because of the influence of Kumarajiva, 90% of the Chinese population became Buddhist. That period came to be known as the 'Second Era of Translator Kumarajiva of Kashmir.'

Recently, the Chinese erected a special monument of Kumarajiva and also instituted a prize for scholars in his name.

## Prince Gunavarman

Prince Gunavarman belonged to the royal family of Kashmir. He entered the Buddhist order at the age of 20. He had mastered all the three divisions of the Buddhist canons. At the age of 30, after the death of the king, he was offered the royal throne but he declined. It is said that he immediately left Kashmir and did not wish to be fettered with kingly duties. As a Buddhist missionary from Kashmir, he was the first traveller to the Southern Asiatic route to China, Korea and Japan to preach the message of Buddha. He also went to Sri Lanka and to Java. Buddhism gained a firm footing in Java because of him. From Java, it spread to Sumatra, well before the 5th century and by the 7th century, the King of Sumatra Srivijaya accepted Buddhism. With the conversion of the royal family to Buddhism, the entire population of the island of Sumatra adopted Buddhism.

In 424 AD, Prince Gunavarman went to China and lectured on Lotus Sutra, the 'Ten Stages Sutra' and other sutras. When Emperor Wen of the Liu Sung Dynasty heard his name and fame, he invited Gunavarman to visit his capital, Chien-k'ang in 431 AD and Gunavarman preached there.

He was a great translator of Buddhist scriptures. During his stay at the Jetavana Monastery, he translated 11 important works into 18 volumes with the collaboration of another Kashmiri scholar Dharmamitra.

Prince Gunavarman was an artist and a painter. As an artist, he followed Kumarajiva to paint *Jataka* stories in public halls in China.

## Virochana

Virochana, another scholar from Kashmir, propagated Buddhism in Khotan and parts of Gandhara and Bamiyan in Afghanistan. Bamiyan was a great centre of Buddhism and was well-known for its giant size Buddha sculptures. The world heritage site was, sadly, destroyed in 2001 by the Taliban to rid Afghanistan of idolatry.

## Meghavahana

Before the advent of the Karkota Dynasty (beginning of the 8th Century), the Gonanda Dynasty gave Meghavahana and Pravansen, two notable rulers to Kashmir. The former was a pious and a strong Hindu ruler with Buddhist leanings. He stopped killing animals and birds, throughout his Kingdom. He undertook the conquest of many countries, solely to stop animal slaughter. His chief queen, Amritaprabha, built 'Amrit Bhawan' Vihara for foreign pilgrims and students who came to Kashmir to study in large numbers.

□

# The Chinese Traveller Husan Tsang in Kashmir

Hsuan Tsang, a Chinese scholar arrived in Kashmir during 631–633 AD, in the reign of King Durlab Vardhan. He entered the valley from *Varahmulla*, where he found a huge stone gate. He was given a royal reception by the Hindu King and treated as a state guest. In his writings, he mentions Kashmir as a flourishing centre of Buddhist culture rivalling Maghada. Hsuan Tsang describes the existence of over 100 monasteries and over 5,000 monks in the area. He has also mentioned that the Fourth Buddhist Council took place in Kashmir. According to his account, nearly 500 Buddhist and Hindu scholars attended the Fourth Buddhist Council. He praises the intellectual calibre of Kashmiri scholars and considered them incomparable. According to him, the entire proceedings of the conference were inscribed in Sanskrit on copper plates and put in stone boxes and deposited in a vihara. Like famous Gilgit manuscripts, these copper plates may be unearthed in the near future.

While in Kashmir, Hsuan Tsang studied the *Sutras, Shastras,* Sanskrit language and the Hindu and Buddhist scriptures with talented Kashmiri Pandit scholars and monks such as Samghayasas and Vinītaprabha, Candravarman and Jayagupta for over two years.

It is said that King Durlabh Vardhan provided him with

20 scribes who copied the religious scriptures for him. The Chief Buddhist scholar of that time declared Hsuan Tsang as one of the greatest scholars in the tradition of Acharya Vasubandhu. Hsuan Tsang was indeed an ancient ambassador of peace between China and India. Even though he visited Kashmir much later, in his accounts, he mentions Emperor Ashoka making the gift of the valley to Buddhist Sangha. Many Buddhist scholars, missionaries and intellectuals permanently settled in the valley during Ashoka's reign.

## Vihara at Ganpatyar Temple

Ganpatyar, the temple of Ganesh where we used to almost go daily for the morning and evening *aartis*, housed a vihara at the time of Hsuan Tsang, where he stayed while in Srinagar. He called it Vrihat Vihara. Presently, the locality is known as Badyar. Hsuan Tsang also mentions a 'Jainder Vihara' in Srinagar, containing a huge Buddha idol where he had stayed. Besides these sites, many places in Kashmir remind us of Buddhism and its influence on Kashmir such as Parihaspora, Anderkut, Ahen (Sumbal), 'Khandhbhawan' in Srinagar, 'Rattani Pura, Harwan, and Vijay Vihara'.

□

# Kashmiri Influence on Buddhist Art and Architecture

The Kashmiri style of Buddhist images moulded in metal appeared in Western Tibet and Ladakh. Kashmiri Buddhist scholars also migrated to Tibet and Iran. Hindu and Buddhist edifices produced in ancient Kashmir were greatly influenced by Hindu and Buddhist iconography. Unfortunately, they have not survived and remain in ruins. Buddhist architecture in Kashmir has three clear divisions- First is the architecture of Harwan. This belongs to the Indo-Parthian style. After that, we see the architecture of Kushan King Hushka in the first century A.D., who raised the city of 'Hushkapur' in Gandhara style. The architectural and sculptural remains found at Pandrethan near Srinagar belong to the Gupta style.

The sculpture of Mahamaya (Buddha's mother) along with her sisters before the birth of Buddha is a significant find of the Gupta period. This sculpture shows Mahamaya wearing an ornament, a long earring (dejeharu) which is worn even today by married Kashmiri Hindu women. This type of ear ornament is supposed to be the influence of the Naga tradition of Kashmir. This shows the influence of local art and culture on Buddhist art.

## The Monasteries of Rinchen Zangpo

The Hindu dated 26th April, 2013 reported that the historian Benoy Behl had made a film documenting monasteries of Rinchen Zangpo undertaking expeditions to the treacherous mountains in Tibet, Lahaul-Spiti, Kinnaur and Ladakh. He has documented the work of the outstanding artists from Kashmir whose paintings and sculptures are testimony to a great tradition of art used in these ancient monasteries. It is worth mentioning how these monasteries came into being.

Lochen Rinchen Zangpo, known as the Mahaguru and a great translator, translated all the important Buddhist works from Sanskrit and Prakrit into Tibetan. He is especially known for the great role he played in 'Second Diffusion of Buddhism in Tibet'. This period is also known as the 'New Translation School Period' or 'New Mantra School Period'.

In the 9th century, Buddhism was in decline in Guge, western Tibet and trans-Himalayas, due to persecution by Bon rulers like Langdarma. They destroyed the monasteries and killed the monks. The territory of Guge then consisted of Ladakh, Spiti, Kinnaur, Guge, Zanskar, Nepal and Puranag in western Tibet. The situation changed when King Yeshe-Ö (947–1024 AD) came to the throne.

Concerned about the downfall of Buddhism, the king sent 22 young scholars to Kashmir to study. He wanted them to learn Sanskrit and understand the true essence of Buddhism. Out of 22, only two survived the harsh journey to Kashmir. The survivors were Rinchen Zangpo and his cousin Lekpai Sherab. While Rinchen Zangpo is known as a great translator, Lekpai Sherab became known as a lesser translator.

Rinchen Zangpo is considered the single most important personality for the 'Second Propagation of Buddhism' in Tibet. He built 108 monasteries in different parts of the Himalayan region including the Tabo monastery in Spiti, Poo monastery in Kinnaur and the Rinchenling monastery in Nepal.

He was ordained as a teenager by a monk called Khenpo Yeshe Zangpo and travelled to India by a royal decree at the age of 13.

His first teacher in Kashmir was Sraddhakara Varman under whom he studied Sanskrit, philosophy, tantric practices and Buddhist scriptures for seven years. The Tibetan sources say he made two more visits to India and in all, studied with 75 Kashmiri Pandits. He learnt Yogatantras from Ratnavajra. He also went to Vikramsila and studied there with Dipankara Bhadra and others.

After returning to Tibet, Rinchen Zangpo and Lekpai Sherab constructed the new royal monastery at Toling. A number of Pandits from Kashmir joined them in translating the Sanskrit texts into Tibetan. He constructed two more temples at that time. He spent another six years visiting Kashmir and other parts of India.

His biography mentions that for building Alchi and other monasteries, he came back to Guge, bringing 32 best Kashmiri Pandit artists to create icons, sculptures and mural paintings connected to the life of Buddha. These artists created over a 100 monasteries which he had mentally visualised stretching on the entire Himalayan region. Of these buildings, a few still survive.

## Kalhana on Alchi Monastery

Historian Kalhana in *Rajatarangini* gives an account of Rinchen Zangpo and monasteries built by him, especially, the best among them, Alchi, situated 10,500 feet above sea level on the banks of the Indus River.

## Alchi Monastery

If one visits the Alchi Monastery in Ladakh, one can see the exquisite artwork created on its walls by the Kashmiri artists 900 years ago. Alchi, crafted by the hands of Kashmiri Pandits is indeed a mixture of Kashmiri, Tibetan and Central Asian artistic traditions.

Benoy Behl through his film has tried to make people aware that it was the Kashmiri artists who painted all monasteries in Himalayan regions. These artists laid the foundation of the later traditions of Buddhism in the trans-Himalayas. Their immense artistic contribution helped in the revival of Buddhism in the region.

Comparing the art in these monasteries with other works of art in the country, Benoy Behl says these are the finest trans-Himalayan pieces of exquisite art in the region and can be compared with the mural art of Ajanta and Thanjavur. Some of these monasteries such as the Sumda monastery is located 12,500 feet above sea level and could be reached only after undertaking an arduous journey.

Even though Buddhism totally disappeared from the valley of Kashmir with the advent of Islam in the 14th century, yet, we can proudly say that the credit for preserving the legacy of Buddhism in Ladakh and Tibet goes to Kashmiri Pandit scholars and artists who made a tremendous contribution.

□

# Jesus in Buddhist Kashmir

One of the mysteries of Srinagar is if Jesus Christ lived and died in Kashmir. According to the local legend, he did. As teenagers,we have visited the tomb of Jesus (Yuz Asaf) at Roza Bal in Khanyar in downtown Srinagar with our elders. Generally, tombs of saints and *rishis* were visited by all the communities irrespective of their religion. The keeper of the tomb, a local man, took us around and showed us the rock in the tomb which contains the impressions of feet bearing the crucifixion marks, supposed to be the impression of the feet of Jesus. That was our early introduction to Roza Bal.

Later in the eighties, we read articles about Jesus being in India. These articles had appeared in the magazine titled Mountain Path published by the Ramana Maharishi's Ashram in Tiruvannamalai. The articles stated that Jesus was in India not once but twice. Once, during the missing years between the age of 13 and 30, he had come to India along with a merchant's caravan and studied Indian and Buddhist philosophies, *Vedas*, *Upanishads* and *Yoga* in Varanasi, Tibet, Nepal and Kashmir.

He returned to Kashmir after his crucifixion and stayed on till he passed away in ripe old age. It is stated that when Christ rose from the dead, he rose from a state of yogic *Samadhi*. Being a yogi of the highest order, he never died; the Romans could not kill him. After rising on Easter Sunday and meeting his disciples and asking them to disperse, he is supposed to have travelled back to India and Kashmir, taught at the Buddhist University at Harvan near Srinagar and died at a ripe old age in Kashmir. He is supposed to be buried in Srinagar in Roza Bal.

According to the legend of the manuscript, a caravan of a rich merchant was passing through the village where Jesus lived. When the merchant spotted a brilliant 13-year old boy with a divine aura, he realised that the young lad was meant for higher purposes. He decided to bring Jesus with him to India to be educated by the great masters and philosophers. That is how Jesus seemed to have travelled with this caravan to India and obtained an education in Eastern philosophies, meditation and yoga. He was a profound yogi. At the right age, he felt the calling to go back to his native land and preach to his people and he made his journey back to Jerusalem.

It is quite possible that Jesus did not die but went merely into *Yoganidra,* the yogic deep sleep or *Samadhi.* When he arose, he decided to come back to India where his non-violent and unconventional philosophies would thrive very well in a Buddhist university and where Kashmiri disciples would listen to him eagerly.

These articles in Mountain Path were based on the accounts of nineteenth-century Russian journalist and adventurer Nicolas Notovitch, who visited Kashmir, Ladakh and Tibet. He accidentally broke his leg and found refuge in a Buddhist monastery in 1894. There he learnt about the story of Jesus's visit to Tibet and Kashmir and was told about the manuscripts in Sanskrit and Pali, which contained the stories about Jesus preserved in important monasteries such as Hemis monastery. He finally made it to Hemis and saw the manuscript which was read to him by monks. He made a record of all that he learnt. He wrote this account in his book titled 'Unknown Life of Jesus Christ'. Unfortunately, after the Chinese occupation of Tibet, these monasteries went into Chinese hands and the fate of these monasteries as well as the wealth of manuscripts stored there is not known. Hence, it is no more possible to verify these manuscripts. Many monasteries and manuscripts were destroyed by the Chinese; so one cannot tell the fate of this manuscript.

A century later, Holger Kersten inspired by Nicolas Notovitch, went to Kashmir and Ladakh and conducted research and then wrote his book 'Jesus Lived in India' in 1993.

When in the nineties, we read Holger Kersten's book 'Jesus Lived in India', it brought back memories of our visit to Roza Bal years ago. Though there is a lot of controversy on the subject, somewhere in our hearts, we feel that accounts of Notovitch and Kersten might be true. The following arguments are given in favour of Jesus's visits to India.

It is said that there is a marked difference in the philosophy of the Old Testament and the New Testament. The God in the first testament is an angry God, a vengeful God and a punishing God. Old Testament preaches 'an eye for an eye' whereas Jesus preaches love, non-violence and compassion which is so close to what Buddha preached. The scholars believe that Jesus came under the influence of eastern philosophies including Buddhism before he went back to preach in Jerusalem at the age of thirty.

Jesus says if someone slaps you on one cheek, give the other cheek also. This is a big departure from the 'eye for eye' philosophy of the Old Testament.

According to Kersten, there are other witnesses both before and after Notovitch who have heard or seen the Tibetan manuscripts. Even forty years before Notovitch's visit to Hemis, a certain Mrs. Hervey has talked about the Tibetan texts and mentions Jesus in her book titled, 'The Adventures of a Lady in Tartary, Thibet, China & Kashmir' which appeared in 1853. Many more have witnessed the relevant documents before they finally disappeared. One of them was Indian holy man Swami Abhedananda born in 1866. Abhedananda studied in Oriental Seminary in Calcutta and later went to England where he met Max Muller. In 1922, he went on a pilgrimage to Tibet. On the way to Tibet, he visited Hemis monastery to verify Notovich's story with the monks. He was taken inside and shown the manuscript and the abbot helped him in translating the text. Till this point, Kersten was sceptical about the claims of Notovitch but when he saw the manuscript, all his doubts vanished.

Kersten further mentions that in 1925, Nicolas Roerich, a Russian painter and archaeologist, who spent many years in India investigated the matter with the people of Ladakh and came to know that the legend of Issa was known to them in various forms and spoke of him with worshipful reverence.

After him, Lady Henrietta Merrick confirmed the existence of the manuscripts in her book titled, 'In the World's Attick' published in 1931 in which she wrote, "In Leh is the legend of Christ who is called Issa. It is said the monastery of Hemis holds precious ancient documents which tell of the days Issa spent in Leh where he was joyously received and where he preached."

In 1939, a Swiss lady named Madame Elizabeth Caspari visited the Hemis Monastery while on pilgrimage to Mount Kailash. The librarian of the monastery showed her the old manuscript.

Nobody has seemed to have seen the manuscript after this time.

Kashmiri writer and supporter of the Ahmadiyya view, Fida Hassnain also refers to the rock with crucifixion marks of Jesus's feet. Besides, he says that the body is buried according to Jewish tradition and not as per Islamic tradition. There has been much controversy on this issue. As per the local tradition, the tomb belongs to an ancient pre-Islamic foreign prophet, Yuz Asaf (Jesus the Gatherer) and has existed for aeons of time. However, when Bulbul Shah, the founder of Islam in Kashmir, visited the tomb in the 14th Century, he declared it to be the tomb of a Muslim Saint. Later, a Muslim saint called Mir Sayyid Naseeruddin was also buried alongside in Roza Bal.

Abdul Aziz Kashmiri has also mentioned this in his book

'Hazrat Isa aur Issayat', in 1954 which was translated into English in 1968.

Andreas Faber-Kaiser a Spanish writer of German descent also wrote 'Jesus Died in Kashmir' in 1977. He also maintained the minority view that Jesus did not die on the cross. He survived the crucifixion, was hidden by Essenes and travelled to India.

After the publication of Kersten's book, the tourist flow to the tomb of Jesus at Roza Bal increased greatly. Currently, we understand tourists are not allowed to visit the tomb. The Roza Bal has been taken over by Sunni Muslim Board from the hands of local caretakers.

□

# Part-3

# Temples and Sacred Places

# Cave of Amarnath Abode of Shiva and Parvati

The holiest of the holy cave shrine of Amarnath is dedicated to Lord Shiva, who is present here in the form of an ice *lingam*.

Before reaching the cave, we have to cross the Panchtarni River. It is believed that those who cross the river are relieved of the cycle of births and deaths. Panchatarni means deliverer from five bondages. It is believed to free one from five sins of vanity, anger, greed, jealousy, and attachment and also from four stages of life and the fifth stage of death. Death is looked upon as a frozen state and the frozen Panchtarni River is a symbol of death. This is the reason that many *sadhus* and sages choose to die at Amarnath. Dying at Amarnath is considered the best way to attain *nirvana*.

In the olden days, the *yatra* used to be very tough. When our ancestors left for the *yatra*, we were not sure if we would see them again. Such were the odds against their safe return that their *shraddha* ceremony and the death rites were performed before they left home.

The hoary and venerated cave of Amarnath has been elaborately discussed in many ancient texts. According to *Shiv Purana*, Amarnath is the site where the dialogue between Shiva and Parvati took place. These dialogues contain the essence of Shaiva philosophy. With the destruction of Hindu manuscripts by the Muslim Sultans and Afghan rulers of Kashmir, these dialogues had gone missing. The ancient dialogues were unearthed by Swami Lakshmanjoo Raina in the 20th century and were published in Paul Reps in his book 'Zen Flesh Zen Bones.'

The pilgrimage to the holy cave with full topographical details is given in the *Bhringish Samhita* and the *Amarnath Mahatmya*. *Nilamata Purana*, a 6th century Sanskrit text which depicts the religious and cultural life of early Kashmir has mentioned the cave in detail.

References to Amarnath have also been made in historical chronicles like *Rajatarangini*, which mentions that the Amarnathshrine has been visited by the kings and commons even before 34 BC.

Jonaraja in his sequel to *Rajatarangini* also gives details of the pilgrimage. The *Rajavalipataka* which was begun by Prajna Bhatta and completed by Shuka makes a clear reference to the pilgrimage to the sacred site. Many Western travellers have also mentioned the holy cave in their accounts. All this goes to show that the holy cave has been in existence for millenniums.

The original name of the sacred spot given in the ancient texts is Amareshwara-the Immortal God. In course of time, it has become Amarnath–the Immortal Lord.

The Amarnath Cave has a special significance in the Hindu religion because Lord Shiva chose this spot to impart the secrets of immortality and the formation of the universe to Parvati. According to the legend, once Parvati asked Shiva, why he was wearing a garland of skulls. To this, Shiva replied, "Whenever you are reborn, a skull is added to the garland. The garland of skulls shows your births and deaths." Parvati further asks–Why are you immortal and why do I keep dying time and again? Shiva replied that it was due to the 'Amar Katha'—the tale of immortality. Parvati insisted on hearing the 'Amar Katha' and after much persuasion, Shiva finally decided to narrate the story to her.

For this purpose, Shiva started looking for a secluded place so that no living being can hear Amar Katha except Parvati. He finally found the cave of Amarnath. To reach this high altitude spot, one by one, he left all his belongings on the way. He left his bull 'Nandi' at Pahalgam which was originally known as 'Bailgam', the village of the bull. He left his Moon at Chandanwari, his snakes at the banks of Sheshnag Lake, his son Ganesha at Mahagunas *Parvat* and he left five elements of Earth, Fire, Water, Air and Sky at Panchtarni River.

After this, Lord Shiva entered the holy Amarnath Cave with Parvati and sat in meditation on deerskin. To make sure that not a single soul heard the secret of Amar Katha, he created a Rudra named Kalagni and ordered Kalagni to set fire around the cave so that every living thing around the cave was destroyed. He then started narrating the story to Parvati. Despite all these efforts, one egg remained protected under the deerskin on which the Lord was sitting. A pair of pigeons was born out of that egg, which became immortal by hearing the Amar Katha. Some lucky pilgrims can see the pair of pigeons at the cave or on the way to the cave. It is a marvel to find these birds at such a high altitude.

The *Bhringesh Samhita* narrates yet another story about Amarnath. It says, once sage Bhrigu was travelling through this region and he saw a cave. He was drawn into the cave and there he was struck with wonder when he saw a huge ice *lingam*. He is said to be the first to have *darshan* of Shiva, in form of an ice *lingam*. He found that the ice *lingam* started growing with the waxing moon in the Hindu month of *Ashada* and reached its full size on the day of the full moon in the month of *Shravana*. This is the day *Raksha Bandhan* is celebrated in north India and *Avani Avittam* is celebrated in south India. The men replace their old sacred thread by wearing a new one in south India. Sage Brigu also found two more small ice lingams in the cave which according to him were symbols of Parvati and Ganesh.

When people heard of this phenomenon from the sage, the cave of Amarnath came to be known as the abode of Shiva and became a great pilgrim centre. Since then lakhs of devotees undertake the annual pilgrimage through tough terrain and attain eternal bliss.

## Story of Sheshnag

Kalhana in *Rajatarangini,* while making mention of the holy cave mentions the legend of Sheshnag, the beautiful lake en-route to Amarnath. It was the abode of the Naga Chief, Naga Sushravas. The Naga Sushravas had given his beautiful daughter in marriage to a Brahmin youth who had helped him in harvesting his crops. However, King Nara, the ruler of Chakradhar near Vijyeshwar, tried to abduct the young Brahman's Naga wife. This aroused the wrath of Naga Sushruvas, who in all blood and fury burnt and destroyed Nara's entire kingdom and put him to death. However, Naga Sushruvas, fearing reprisals from the king's relatives, took his daughter and son-in-law to his abode at 'Sushram Nag' which is now known as Sheshnag. Kalhana describes the Sheshnag Lake as 'the lake of dazzling whiteness resembling a sea of milk'.

The cave was visited and patronised by many queens and kings. It is believed that Queen Suryamathi in the 11th century AD gifted tridents *banalingas* and other sacred emblems to the cave temple.

In his Chronicles of Kashmir, Jonaraja relates that Sultan Zain-ul-Abidin paid a visit to the sacred spot of Amarnath while inspecting a canal being constructed on the left bank of the Lidder River.

## Inspiration to Meet Guru Tegh Bahadur

Kashmiris got some respite from forced conversion during the reign of Akbar but things changed in the later Mughal period. Aurangzeb and his cruel governor Iftikhar Khan, once again subjected the Kashmiri Pandits to forced conversion to Islam, through the worst ever persecution and torture. At that time, 500 Kashmiri Pandits under the astute leadership of Kirpa Ram Dutt, a Shaivite Scholar, met at the Holy cave to devise a strategy to meet the challenge. One of them had a vision of Lord Shiva directing him to go and meet Guru Tegh Bahadur at the Shri Anandpur Sahib in Punjab and seek his help. It was from the Holy cave of Amaranth that Kirpa Ram Dutt in obedience to Lord Shiva led the delegation of 500 Pandits to Guru Tegh Bahadur. Everyone knows about the sacrifice of Guru Teg Bahadur for saving Hindu dharma and the formation of *Khalsa Panth* by his son Guru Gobind Singh.

## Rediscovering the Cave

During the rule of Sultans and Afghans, Hindus could not go on holy pilgrimage and the cave remained abandoned for several centuries. The route to the cave was lost. There is an interesting legend about the rediscovery of the route. Once a Muslim chief of the *Bakarwal* clan lost his herd of sheep and went climbing higher and higher till he reached the cave. An amazing sight greeted him there. He saw a very handsome man with a serpent around his neck, and a divinely beautiful woman sitting on a bull. Despite being dazed to see them, he asked them if they had seen his sheep. They told him that his herd of sheep had reached home. They also touched the sack of firewood he was carrying on his back and told him to return home. Before leaving, he saw them disappearing into the cave. At home, he found his herd of sheep had returned and when his wife opened the sack of firewood, she found gold bars instead of firewood.

Astonished by this miracle, he went down to the Hindu village of Ganeshpuri and narrated the experience to the Pandits there. Having heard the story, they conclude that *Bakarwal* had encountered none other than Lord Shiva, Parvati and Nandi at the cave of Amarnath and requested to be taken there. The *Bakarwal* chief led them to the cave where they saw an ice *linga* and a pair of pigeons. This way, the route to the cave was found again. From that day on, the Pandits of Ganeshpuri tend to the shrine and act as priests and Muslim Bakarwals guard the pathway and guide pilgrims. Both these communities share the proceeds from the shrine.

Over the last two centuries, the holy cave has again become a major pilgrim destination. It is believed that the Sikh Guru Arjan Dev granted land in Amritsar for the ceremonial departure of *Chhari*, the holy mace of Lord Shiva which marks the beginning of the pilgrimage to the Holy Cave. Shri Samsar Chand Kaul in his 'Mysterious Cave of Amarnath' mentions that after the Afghan rule ended in 1818, Pandit Hardas Tiku founded the 'Chhawni Amarnath' at Ram Bagh in Srinagar. The *sadhus* and pilgrims from the plains assembled there and were assisted in the journey from his private resources.

Swami Vivekananda undertook a pilgrimage to Amarnath in 1889. Even now, the Mace of Shiva is carried ceremonially each year from Dashnami Akhada in Srinagar and *sadhus* travelling on foot in a procession carry the mace of Shiva to the holy cave.

It is our wish that our children should know the spiritual

might of the place they belong to. They must know the cultural richness and values of their ancestral place and the divine blessings they will carry with them as long they do not break the umbilical cord. Let Mahadev Shiva continue to bestow his blessings upon them.

*Excerpts from Nilamata Purana, Rajatarangini, Vanamali Ashram writings etc.*

□

# Sharada Peeth and Sharada Mata Temple

Goddess Saraswati is venerated as Goddess Sharada in Kashmir and is the presiding deity of Kashmir. Her temple is located at Sharda Gram in the Dhrov region in Pakistan occupied Kashmir, on the banks of the Krishna Ganga (also known as Kishanganga) River. The temple represents the spiritual soul of Kashmir. In the hymns dedicated to Sharada, she is always identified as Kashmir Vasini, the resident of Kashmir. Goddess Sharada is a part of the native identity of Kashmir and represents the heritage of its belief system. The authority of the goddess over the entire Kashmir constitutes the pillar of our folklore. It is due to her overpowering presence that Kashmir is known as 'Sharada Mandal', 'Sharada Desh', 'Sharada Peeth' and Sharada Van.

This most sacred Sharada Peeth is said to be the place where the right hand of Sati fell when Shiva was wandering crazily carrying Sati's corpse after she committed suicide by jumping into the fire in her father's house. As per folklore, Lord Krishna is believed to have visited the place to meet the Pandavas during their wanderings in exile. The local river was named Krishna Ganga to commemorate Lord Krishna's visit. According to the legend, Lord Rama, Sita and Lakshmana have also visited Sharadi Gram during their exile.

As goddess of knowledge, intellect and exalted thoughts,

Sharada is believed to be present wherever speech and communication exist. She is Vaksavitri, the creator of all types of communication, particularly spiritual knowledge. In ancient times, this abode of Goddess Saraswati, the Sharada Peeth was a renowned centre of learning and an ancient university contemporary to the University in Taxila, meaning the 'city of carved stone', in present-day Punjab in Rawalpindi in Pakistan.

The Sharada Peeth University was visited by the famous Chinese Buddhist scholar, Hiuen Tsang about 1,400 years ago. Nagasena and Kumarajiva, ancient Buddhist scholars, were also connected with the University. Al Beruni, the Arab historian who lived 1,000 years ago, mentions the temple and the image of the goddess within. Historian Kalhana has also described Sharada Peeth in *Rajatarangini*. It is said that Ramanujacharya of South visited this temple before he wrote his commentary on Vedanta. The Jain scholar Hemachandra did reference work in Sharada Peeth while writing his treatise on grammar.

It is believed that the temple had a wooden image of the goddess. It was later replaced with a stone statue, akin to the Sharada image installed at Shringeri by Adi Shankaracharya. In the image of Shringeri, the goddess has four arms. On one hand, she holds a parrot (symbol of Parvati), in the second hand, she holds a pot (symbol of Lakshmi), in the third hand, she holds a book (symbol of Saraswati) and her fourth hand is in 'Varda mudra' with which she bestows knowledge.

Today, in place of a great centre of learning, we simply have stone walls and ruins. The archaeologists believe that Sharada Peeth could have existed even before the dawn of the Christian era, and was destroyed by Sikandar Butshikan who used brute force to establish Islam in Kashmir. With that, an ancient university with all its archives of manuscripts and scriptures was destroyed and abandoned. After a few centuries, the temple was partially restored by Maharaja Gulab Singh in the 19th century. Since then, regular pilgrimage to the Sharada Peeth restarted, which continued till 1947. In 1947, the site came under Pakistan occupied Kashmir and fell into disuse as no pilgrims could visit it anymore. The lone Pandit family which looked after the temple as well as conducted the *pujas* was forced to leave. An earthquake in 2005 seems to have further damaged the structure.

There has been no pilgrimage to the Sharada Mata temple after August 1947. There is a need to take up the matter at the diplomatic level with the concerned authorities and restart the pilgrimage and rebuild the temple of Goddess Sharada.

□

# Martand Sun Temple—A Possible Landing Zone for Space Travellers

Erich von Daniken sold over 40 million books presenting his theories that the Earth was visited by extra-terrestrials some 10,000 to 40,000 years ago. As evidence, Von Daniken points to the countless legends seen in cultures around the world that tell of winged gods or flying machines. According to him, these are inspired, not by flights of fancy in the teller's mind, but by actual visits down through the ages of aliens with their advanced technology. For more tangible proof, Von Daniken points to archaeological oddities found around the world including the Great Pyramids of Egypt, the famous mysterious lines in Peru's Nazca and the colossal Sun Temple at Martand amongst others.

His theory is most intriguing about the glorious Sun Temple of Martand. In his book 'The Chariots of the Gods', he is convinced that it was a place for the landing of space travellers.

We are not surprised at Eric Von's belief. For a land as ancient as Kashmir with spirituality and mysticism in its roots, there are numerous mysteries and legends connected with it.

The Sun Temple at Martand is the most memorable and beautiful work of King Lalitaditya. It is the largest Hindu temple in Kashmir. The emperor built it in the honour of the

Sun God Bhaskar. The King himself was a Kshatriya of the Sun Dynasty. This historic temple was started by Ramaditya in the 5th century probably between 490 and 555 AD. The style of the construction of the temple and the skill exhibited in its construction is rare in the history of the world. Though the cities, towns and the ruins belonging to the era of Lalitaditya are not to be found so easily, the remnants of the big Martand temple, despite the hard demolishing work of Sikandar Butshikan, still stand majestically. Their sheer existence is an example of the unique building skill of the ancient Kashmiri Pandits who are praised for their design, beauty and art by many.

Sir Francis Edward Younghusband in his book 'KASHMIR' writes, "Martand has a very high place in the world's great architectural designs. It is an example of not only the Kashmiri architectural skill but it has the pride of having been set up at a fine spot which is prettier than the spots where Parthenon, Taj Mahal, St. Peters Church, have been built. It can be considered either a representative of all such great buildings and monuments or a combination and sum total of all their qualities. It gives an insight into the greatness of the people of Kashmir. In terms of beauty and strength and grandeur, it is next to Egypt and Greece. It is now in ruins and there are many such ruins scattered in Kashmir. The very existence of this temple encourages man to carry out a study of the skill and art of Kashmiris. Anyone bereft of the love of nature could not select such a special spot for the construction of the temple.

The temple turns out to be the largest example of a peristyle and is complex due to its various chambers that are proportional in size and aligned with the overall perimeter of the temple. The entrance is highly reflective of the temple as a whole due to its elaborate decoration and allusion to the deities worshipped inside. The primary shrine is located in a centralised structure (the temple proper) that is thought to have had a pyramidal top, a common feature of the temples in

Kashmir. Various wall carvings in antechamber of the temple proper depict other gods, such as Vishnu, river goddesses Ganga and Yamuna, in addition to the sun-god Surya.

Many three-faced Vishnu and some *Chaturbhuja* Vishnu figures have been prominently carved on the walls of the temple. A central water tank with narrow water channels exists to this day. The right panel of the eastern wall of the antechamber depicts Aruna carved discerningly as the charioteer of Surya and is holding the reins of the seven horses of Surya.

Martand temple is said to be a mirror of the art and skill of Kashmiri Pandits. King Lalitaditya should not only be considered a founder of a vast empire but also the greatest promoter of the art and architecture of Kashmir.

Guru Nanak Dev visited this holy place in 1500 during his pilgrimage to Kashmir.

We end with a few lines from Muriel Talbot's poem, written in the glory of Martand:

*The Martand Temple*
*Still eloquent of prayers, though stones decay,*
*And forms of ancient creeds have passed away.*

*The Sun's pure glory is God's symbol bright.,*
*Thus thy great destiny can never end:*
*Temple of the Sun! High radiant beam.*

*Illustration of Martand Temple by J. Duguid around 1870, giving a majestic view of the temple as it would have been before its demolition by Sikandar Butshikan.*

□

# Zethyar Kashmir—The Abode of Shakti

In Kashmir, the worship of Mother Goddess is universal. She is worshipped as Uma, the part of Shiva and as Shakti in the form of Sharika. As Ragnya, she is worshipped as the nurturer of the universe and as Sharada or Saraswati, she is worshipped as the consciousness of knowledge. She is the manifestation of energy as Jwalaji. In the form of Mahakali, she is an expression of the absolute time or the *Kala*. As Tripurasundari, she is known as Bala Devi. She is also worshipped in the form of Bhima Devi, Beda Devi, Ganga and Vitasta.

As Bhadrakali, she is the embodiment of Kali, who came from Bengal in pursuit of demons and destroyed them in the village of Wadipora, in Handwara. In Kashmir, she is also worshipped as Zyestha Devi, the form of Shakti created by Shiva to rescue Goddess Lakshmi, who was abducted by the *Asuras* during the churning of the ocean.

The cult of Devi is so strong in Kashmir that every family has a Kuladevi.. Its genesis lies in the fact that once the valley of Kashmir was a lake called Satisar, the lake of the Sati, the consort of Shiva. It was converted into its present form by Rishi Kashyap through his penance and prayers to Goddess Parvati and Lord Shiva. This Shakti Peetha of Kashmir is blessed by all the three Goddesses, namely, Goddess Sharika who has her abode at Hari Parbhat in Srinagar, Goddess Tripurasundari, also known as Ragnya Bhagwati or Goddess Kheer Bhawani who resides in the holy spring at Tulumulla and the Goddess Zyestha, who has her abode on the banks of Dal Lake at Zabarvan hills opposite the Shankaracharya Hills in Srinagar. The most important thing about these three Shakti Peethas is that they are equidistant from each other and form a triangle, symbolic of Sri Chakra comprising of the two triangles making a star. Each Kashmiri Pandit family owes allegiance to one of three Goddesses as their family deity or *Kuladevi.*

Zyestha Devi is the eldest *(zyeshta)* of them all and a very ancient Goddess. Her shrine seems to have existed for over three thousand years. It is the oldest temple in Kashmir existing from the time of the Pandavas and Mahabharata as well as during the time of Ashoka. A big temple was built by King Gopaditya in the 6th century which was renovated by King Lalitaditya in the 8th Century.

That grand temple does not exist anymore due to the devastation of all temples in Kashmir. Today, we only see a humble shrine in the middle of magnificent natural surroundings. A Shivalinga originally belonging to Ganpatyar Temple in the old city of Srinagar was relocated here for safety in 1988. The Shivalinga was under the threat of destruction by militants.

The origin of Zyeshta Devi relates to an important event that took place during the churning of the ocean, the *Kshirasagara*. Boththe *Devas* and *Asuras* were desirous of obtaining nectar for attaining immortality. They needed the permission of Lord Shiva for the churning of the ocean. Both the groups with great reverence worshipped Lord Shiva who permitted them to churn the ocean on the condition that whatever substance came out from the ocean would be shared by both the *Devas* and *Asuras* equally. Unaware of the nature of the substance that would come out from the ocean, they gladly accepted the condition.

Having obtained the permission, they were still puzzled, as to how to accomplish the churning of such a huge ocean. Disappointed, they again approached Lord Shiva for bestowing them with divine power which would make it possible. Lord Shiva advised them to use the Mandara Mountain-the biggest mountain, as the churner, appeal to Lord Vishnu to take the incarnation of a giant tortoise, Kurmadevta to hold the Mandara Mountain on his back and request the King of serpents, Vasuki for offering his body to be used as the churning rope.

Having thus obtained the help of Mount Mandara, Lord Vishnu and Vasuki, the *Devas* and *Asuras* started the process of churning. Suddenly, the ocean started emitting lethal poison called Halahala– which could destroy the entire universe instantaneously.

Being of a very virulent character, it started engulfing and burning everything up. It was beyond the power of the *Devas* and *Asuras* to control it. In desperation, they begged Lord Shiva to come to their rescue. Lord Shiva, who is *Trilokanatha,* protector of the three worlds, consumed the poison to save the universe. Parvati Devi stopped the poison from going below Shiva's throat. Thus Shiva came to be known as Nilakantha.

The *Devas* and *Asuras* obtained many gems and gifts gems from the ocean and one of them was Goddess Lakshmi.

The *Devas* presented Goddess Lakshmi to Lord Vishnu. This infuriated the *Asuras*. In their anger, they abducted Lakshmi and kept her in captivity in a cave called 'Guptagara'. Currently, this place is known as Gupkar.

This act of the *Asuras* gave rise to the wrath of Shiva. With his divine power, he created Goddess Zyestha and Vira Vaitala with powers to annihilate all the *Asuras* and free Lakshmi from their clutches. Upon accomplishment of the task, Lord Shiva by his grace bestowed upon them the power to protect and uplift mankind. Since then, the devotees of Zyestha Devi are fully protected and obtain the constant grace of the Mother. She is also a protector from all-natural calamities and disasters. It has been a tradition to make an offering of *tehar* and *Charvan* on Thursdays during the month of Zyesth.

This mother's shrine is a place for attaining peace of mind along with getting boons of *Siddhi, Riddhi and Buddhi.* Sri Kanchi Kamakoti Peeth often organises *havan* in the temple for the welfare of inhabitants in this part of the world. Pierre Sonnerat a French naturalist and explorer, who travelled deep into southeast Asia, China, India and Kashmir between 1769 and 1781, has documented the worship of Zeshtha Devi of Kashmir in his book. He has made her drawings and documented other names of Zyestha Mata as Moudevi and as Kakkaikkodiyal, in Tamil. As Kakaikkodiyal, she is shown carrying the banner of the crow and riding a donkey.

We Kashmiri Pandits wherever we live in exile and our coming generations must continue the practice of worshipping the Mother in all her manifestations. Let us keep emphasising with our children, to continue the worship of our *Isht Devis* and keep reminding them about ' Shakti', the creative aspect of the 'Absolute', the symbol of Cosmic Energy. We must continue to worship the divine Mother in Her manifestation of intelligence, discrimination, psychic power and will forever and obtain from Her the power to bounce back.

*Excerpts from Shri C.L. Gadoo's article.*

□

# Tulmul—Shrine of Mata Kheer Bhawani

Worshipping Mother Goddess Kheer Bhawani is universal in Kashmir. The shrine is situated 14 kilometres from Srinagar in the village of TulMu1. The shrine complex is situated around a sacred spring, in a picturesque spot surrounded by Chinar trees. The word `Kheer Bhawani' is made of two words, *kheer* referring to sweet rice pudding that is offered to the goddess and Bhawani meaning Devi. Goddess Kheer Bhawani in Tulmul is a form of Durga and is known by many names, such as Maharagnya, Ragnya, Rajni and even Tripura. Here she appears in her *satvik* form and represents tranquillity and bliss.

According to legend, Goddess Ragnya was pleased with Ravana's devotion and appeared before him. Ravana got an image of the Goddess installed in Sri Lanka. After a while, the goddess became displeased with the unethical life of Ravana and did not wish to stay in Sri Lanka anymore. After Rama vanquished Ravana, he worshipped the goddess and she instructed him to take her out of Sri Lanka. Lord Rama then requested Hanuman to relocate her image from Sri Lanka and install it at a holy spot. Hanuman relocated the shrine of the goddess at Shadipora in Kashmir. Later, Ragnya Devi appeared in the dream of Raghunath Gadroo, a priest, and asked him to shift her shrine from Shadipora to TulMul.

It is said that before handing over the image to Hanuman, Rama worshipped Goddess Ragnya for the last time at Devipattinam near Rameshwaram. Devipattinam in Tamil Nadu is an important Ramayana site of the country. We were delighted to find that the Devi, whom Rama worshipped in Tamil Nadu, was our own Kheer Bhawani. Hence no other image in India can be considered as sacred as that of Kheer Bhawani as it has been worshipped by Lord Rama himself. This story was personally narrated to us by the last hereditary Chief Priest of Devipattinam, Shri Jagannathan lyengar. He also told us that when Paramacharya of Kancheepuram visited Devipattinam, he conducted a special pooja for Devi here. The temple is on the sea shore and it is the only place in India where *navagrahas*, nine planets are located inside the ocean in the form of *navapashanam* (nine stones). A devotee has to stand in the sea to propitiate the *navagrahas*.

The sanctum of Rameshwaram temple possesses the *shivalinga*, worshipped by Rama while returning from Sri Lanka with Sita. It is the only other shrine in India, which carries equal importance. The *shivalinga* in Rameshwaram was crafted by Sita from the sand of the ocean for worship by Rama.

In Sri Lanka, Devi was also known as Shyama. The night on which the Mother Goddess arrived in Kashmir from Sri Lanka is known as the Ragnya Ratri in Kashmir. Several shrines dedicated to the Mother Goddess exist at Tiker, Bhuvaneshvar, Manzgam, Bheda, Mani-gam, Rai-than and Baed-pur. These are the places through which Hanuman passed, en-route to Kashmir. However, the shrine at TulMul is the most powerful. The Ragnya Mahatmya says that those who meditate on Panch Dashi Mantra during *Navreh,* Mother Ragnya would grant their wish.

The shrine was destroyed by Muslim rulers and remained unsung and forgotten for centuries. Following that, due to many floods in Kashmir, the sacred spring of TulMul got denuded and could not be traced anymore. At last, Yogi Krishna Joo Taploo of Srinagar had a dream, in which the goddess directed him to come to a marshy place where she would swim in the form of a water snake and guide him to the exact spot where she abides. She directed him to stick large poles to demarcate the holy spot in the marshland. Subsequently, when the water subsided, the holy spot was discovered. Shri Krishna Joo Taploo possessed valuable manuscripts like *Bhrigu Samhita* which were taken away from his family during the militancy. An annual Havan took place at his residence, coinciding with the discovery of the holy spring. This was later continued by his descendants till the forced migration of Kashmiri Pandits. His descendant, Shri Anil Taploo, resides at Dilshad Garden in Delhi.

In 1912, during the Dogra rule, Maharaja Pratap Singh rebuilt a humble shrine on the spot. It was later renovated by Maharaja Hari Singh. The image of Ragnya Devi is placed in a small shrine made in white marble. The goddess is represented in the form of a natural hexagonal spring that is worshipped by the devotees. According to the legend, originally 360 springs (nagas) surrounded the mainspring but all of these seem to have disappeared as the land has become marshy all around.

## Mela Kheer Bhawani

An annual festival is celebrated on the occasion of Shukla Paksha Ashtami in the month of Jyeshta. The devotees from far and near come to pay homage to the goddess. They observe a fast and conduct a Maha-Yagna in honour of Devi.

## The Change in Colour of the Spring

On this day, the spring changes its colour as per the wishes of the goddess. The changing colour of the water in the spring is viewed as the change in the moods of the goddess. The colour of the water can turn to white, green, brown, grey, blue, violet and even black. The bright green and blue colours signify prosperity.

In 1886, Walter Lawrence, the then British Settlement Commissioner for land, reported the water of the spring to have a violet tinge. The colour of water turning into shades of black is supposed to be a signal of approaching disaster. Some people say that before the exodus of the Pandits from Kashmir in 1990, the colour of the water had turned completely black.

## Mention in Rajatarangini and Aaini-Akbari

The holy spring is mentioned by Kalhana in *Rajatarangini*. He writes that the spring was situated in TulMul on marshy grounds and cited the name of the spring as Mata Ragini Kund. He also mentions that the Brahmins of Kashmir worship this spring and pilgrims from every corner of the country come to have *darshan* of the goddess. He regards the Brahmins of TulMul as noted for their spiritual prowess.

Abul-Fazl, in his book *Aaini-Akbari*, mentions the area of TulMul extending over a region of a hundred *bighas* of land, which sank in the marshy lands during the summer season. He also noted the change in the colour of the water in the spring. Swami Rama Tirtha and Swami Vivekananda also visited the shrine to have *the darshan* of Goddess Ragnya and noted the change in the colour of the water in the holy spring.

□

# Mount Harmukh and Harmukh Gosain

Mount Harmukh, overlooking the Gangabal Lake is part of the Himalayan range and is located between Nallah Sindh in the South and Kishanganga River in the North.

The mountain is sacred to Hindus. For them, it is the abode of Lord Shiva. For the same reason, it is also known as Kailash of Kashmir. It is called Harmukh because its peak appears the same from all four sides.

Harmukh is also known as 'Butsar' which is the corruption of the Sanskrit word 'Bhuteshwara', the lord of the universe, another name for Lord Shiva. Its peak and glory have been mentioned in the ancient *Nilamat Purana*.

About a hundred years ago, Sir Walter Lawrence, recorded in his book, *Valley of Kashmir* that there is a belief that there are mines of gems and rubies at Harmukh. Another local belief is that wherever the the Harmukh peak is visible in the Valley, the serpents of that place happen to be quite harmless. On the other hand, wherever the peak is not visible, the serpents of that locality are poisonous and their bites are fatal.

The beautiful Gangabal Lake, situated at the foot of Mount Harmukh is as important as the Ganges for performing the ancestral rites. That is the reason that the lake is called Gangabal.

In the bright fortnight (the *Shukla Paksha*) of the Hindu month of *Bhadrapada,* Kashmiri Pandits immerse the ashes of their dead in Gangabal Lake and perform their *Shraddha* ceremony.

The glory of Harmukh is sung and the blessings of the Lord of Harmukh are invoked through Kashmiri *Vanvun*—the sacred Vedic hymns sung during weddings and sacred thread ceremonies.

Many devotional songs have been composed in praise of the Lord of Harmukh. The most popular of them is:

*Harmukh Bartal Zagay Madaano*
*Yi Dapaham tee lagayo*....... meaning:
*I will wait at the gates of Harmukh*
*for you my beloved*
*Whatever you ask, I will offer*
*If you ask for lavender*
*I will offer you rose, my beloved*
*Whatever you ask, I will offer*
*Cotton and fire have become one*
*Oh god my heart is stuck on you*
*I can't bear distance from you, anymore*
*Whatever you ask, I will offer.*

Shamas Faqir, a Kashmiri Muslim Sufi poet also composed verses referring to Harmukh and Harmukh Gosain 'the Hermit of Harmukh' as below:

*Zaan'e w'ale kar zaanee yaar,*
*Harmukh Vi'chu Deedar*
*Pard'e Zaal Aaz dard-e-naar,*
*Harmukh Vi'chu Deedar*
Meaning, like the hermit of Harmukh,
"Oh seeker of truth, know the truth,
Turn to Harmukh and see,
Burn the veil, of ignorance today,
on the pain of fire,
Turn to Harmukh and realise"

## The Legend of Harmukh Gosain

The legend of the Harmukh Gosain has been narrated by Professor C.L. Sadhu in his book *Some Marvels of Kashmir*.

According to the legend, once a hermit (*gosain*) tried to reach the summit of Mount Harmukh to meet Lord Shiva face to face to attain *nirvana*. For twelve long years, he tried to scale the summit but did not succeed. One day, he saw a *gujjar* descending from the summit. The hermit approached him and enquired what he encountered on the top.

The *gujjar* who had gone up in search of his goats replied that he had seen a couple milking a cow and drinking its milk out of a human skull. They had offered some milk to him, which he refused to drink, so they rubbed a little milk on his forehead. As soon as *gujjar* indicated the spot on his forehead where the milk was rubbed, the hermit became extremely joyful and rushed to lick *gujjar's* forehead.

It is said that by doing so, the hermit instantly attained *nirvana* and disappeared from the sight to the utter surprise of the *gujjar*. The Harmukh Gosain had finally succeeded in his goal and reached Shiva. Our parents, grandparents and elders always give the example of Harmukh Gosain as one who never gave up saying, *"Zan Chu Yohoy Harmokhuk Gosain."*

Harmukh was first scaled by Thomas Montgomerie in 1856. The pilgrimage to Harmukh takes place once a year on the day of Ganga Ashtami and the *yatra* starts from Narnag.

□

# Harwan—The abode of Mata Bhuvaneshwari—Queen of the Universe

Kalhana maintains in his *Rajatarangini* that there is not a piece of land, equal to a mustard seed that is not sacred in Kashmir. One such sacred place is Harwan. It is located about three kilometres beyond the famous Shalimar garden where a Buddhist monastery existed and the famous Bodhisatva, the glorious Nagarjuna once lived. The place was called Sadarhadvana which stands for the forest of six saints. On a nearby hillock, called Chandpora, connected with Raja Harishchandra, known for his honesty, some ancient ruins still exist.

The Mahadev Mountain believed to be the abode of Lord Shiva overlooks Harwan. It is believed that Lord Shiva keeps a vigil from Mahadev Peak.

In Chandpora, there is a small sacred spring associated with Mata Bhuvaneshwari. Kalhana has mentioned this spring in the *Rajatarangini* which had the idols of Goddess Bhuvaneshwari installed on two of its corners. The spring has sprouted from the hollow of Chinar trees. The water of the main spring at the shrine has curative powers. The legend is that once the only son of a woman had gone blind. Reposing his trust in the kindness of the Goddess Bhuvaneshwari, he washed his eyes with the water of the holy spring for seven consecutive days. He regained his vision through the grace of the Goddess.

The word Bhuvaneśwari is a compound of two words Bhuvana +Iśwari, meaning queen or the ruler of the universe. The Divine Mother is the sovereign of all three worlds. She is also known as Adi Parashakti, one of the earliest forms of Shakti. She is capable of changing situations according to her will and wish. Even the *Navagrahas* (nine planets) and *Trimurtis* cannot stop her activities.

Goddess Bhuvaneshwari is the youngest of the seven divine sisters, the other six being Ragyna, Sharika, Jawala, Zeshta, Uma and Shardha. According to Kashmir Shaivism, Shiva, who is the male counterpart of the Shakti, is the Supreme Being. He remains introvert and dormant, while Shakti is active and dynamic. In her diverse manifestations, Shakti performs manifold functions. As Saraswati, she propagates knowledge and wisdom. As Lakshmi, she distributes wealth and as Kali, she destroys the demons. However, Bhuvaneshwari is adored as eternal Shakti.

In Hinduism, Bhuvaneśwari is the fourth of the ten Mahavidya goddesses and an aspect of Durga as elements of the physical cosmos, in giving shape to the creation of the World. There is an interesting story about her birth. In the beginning, only the Sun God 'Surya' was the master of the sky. The sages and seers begged him to create more worlds and offered prayers and ambrosia to please him. Lord Surya used his Supreme Energy to create other worlds -*lokas* or *bhuvans*. This Supreme Energy manifested in the shape of the great cosmic deity 'Bhuvaneshwari'.

The devotees have deep-rooted faith in Mata Bhuvaneshwari. It is said that when a *havan* was performed to propitiate the Goddess Bhuvaneshwari, on the seventh day, a beautiful snake, bearing white patches, emerged from the spring at Chandpora. It made seven circumambulations around the temple to the joy of the devotees present. It accepted the

milk that was offered to it by the devotees and then vanished. The devotees took it as a good omen, believing firmly that Bhuvaneshwari had blessed them.

The devotees of Mata make only vegetarian offerings to her in the shape of fruits and other edible things. Non-vegetarian offerings to the Goddess are strictly forbidden.

It was the late Swami Lakshmanjoo, renowned saint and Shaivite Scholar, who took care of the shrine of the Goddess.

After the displacement of the Kashmiri Pandits, the preservation and maintenance of the shrine needs attention.

*Excerpts from Shri Chander Mohan Bhat's article and India Divine Movement.*

□

# Kounsar Nag

Kounsar Nag is a high altitude oligotrophic lake formed out of melting snow. It is located at an elevation of 13,000 feet above sea level in the Pir Panchal range in the Kulgam District of Kashmir. The lake is 3 km long and .75 km at its widest point.

It is believed that Manu's boat that carried the Vedas and the *Saptarishis* came to halt near this lake at Naubandhana, after the great flood.

The place bears the footprints of Lord Vishnu and is also known as *Vishnupada.* It is one of the two places in Kashmir Valley associated with *Vishnupada*, another being in Verinag.

Rigveda verse I22.17 mentions three steps of Vishnu. According to Shakyamuni, Vishnu took three steps, one step on earth as fire, the second step in the atmosphere as lightning and the third step in the sky as the sun.

The stories about a hill bearing the footprints of Vishnu were current from the days of Vyasa. The epic *Mahabharata* carries as many as six references to *Vishnupada*, three of which speak of it being on the top of a northern alpine mountain. Historian Suvira Jaiswal says, "At present, we cannot determine its exact location, it appears to have been in the north."

Kalhana in *Rajatarangini* mentions the fabled lake as it as Karam Sar Tirth. Kounsar Nag is also the place where

Hindu Trinity held a council to obtain Kashmira for Kashyap Rishi. Legend says that Rishi Kashyapa wanted to reclaim *Kashyapver* out of the Satisar Lake. He practised penance and invoked the blessings of Brahma, Vishnu and Mahesh. Thereafter, the trinity held a council on the mountain. The trinity is present here in form of the three mountain peaks known as the Shankara, Hari and Brahma peaks. It is said after the deliberations, Vishnu summoned his engineer Balbhadra who made a hole in the mountain with his plough, near Baramulla and the water of the lake ebbed out creating the valley of Kashmir.

Kounsar Nag or *Vishnupada* lies at the base of these mountain peaks. To reach the lake, one will have to trek about two Kilometres. The shape of the lake is exactly like a right foot with five toes and a heel. It is believed, whoever after taking bath in the lake, visualises the three peaks, will find a place in heaven.

Even the sinners are freed of their sins by having *darshan* of these peaks. Different places on the peaks are venerated as hermitages of Brahma, Kashyap, Mahadeva, Ananta, Sun, Moon and Hari. Mahadev's hermitage is located on the spot where Vishnu stood and obtained the victory. Hari's hermitage is celebrated as Narasimha.

Kalhana in *Rajatarangini* mentions the fabled lake as Kramsaras*Tirtha*. Little is known about how Kramsaras Lake came to be called Kounsar Nag. Since the lake is also the abode of the Naga Kaundinya, the place became famous by the name Kaundinya Sar. There is a probability that over a period of time, it became Kounsar.

Kashmiri Pandits hold the lake in great veneration as they believe that God is present during *Bhadon Shuklapaksha Ekadashi* here. As per Naubandhana Mahatmya, the pilgrimage used to take place on the 11th day of the bright fortnight of the Hindu month of *Bhadrapad.* By doing *Tarpan* in this place, pilgrims can get rid of their sins and by beholding the peaks earn a place in heaven. It is also a venerated place for performing the *shraddha* ceremony for ancestors.

Before Kashmiri Pandits forcible exile, the village had 25 Pandit families living there. Except for one family, all were Rainas. The grandfather of Mansa Ram Raina, who hailed from Rainawari, had come here during the latter half of the Afghan rule. Sahaj Ram Raina, who lived here in the 19th century, was an ascetic of great merit. There is a small spring named 'Thaal Nagin' in the Pandit *mohalla.* During old times, as per the legend, *thalis* would come out of spring whenever any request was made. The water of 'Thaal Nagin' is ice-cold in summer and warm in winter.

Sultan Zain-ul-Abidin, the monarch of Kashmir visited Kounsar Nag in 1463 AD. He was so fascinated by the lake that he constructed its replica 'Zaina Sar' in Pampore so that every Kashmiri could experience what a great wonder Kounsar Nag was. He along with his two sons Haji and Behram, visited Kounsar Nag, accompanied by two historians, Srivara and Sinha Bhatta. Srivara has given a graphic description of King's visit. Srivara writes that it took them three days to reach the lake and has recorded:

"Sultan derived untold bliss by seeing the charming Kounsar Nag, stamped with the image of the foot of Lord Vishnu. He made obeisance at the foot of Naubandhana. Observing plentiful streams coming down the mountain with a darkish hue of musk coloured flowers afforded immense pleasure to the Sultan. The Sultan boarded a boat, rowed by five boatmen, taking me and Sinha Bhatta along, roamed deep into the lake. I recited songs from Gita-Govinda to him and Sultan derived great aesthetic pleasure from the songs. While roaming in the lake, it began to snow. The Sultan made three rounds around the lake. Afterwards, the king strolled around the lake and kept describing to the princes, the great beauty of Kounsar Nag." In his time, Naubandhana pilgrimage was quite popular.

We can understand this when we observe the charm and beauty of this unique high altitude lake. Sitting on its shore, the whole day, and watching it change colours as rays from the angular height of the sun reflect on the surface of the lake, the Kounsar Nag fills our mind with awe and wonder. The Tarsar Lake in the Lidder Valley has a soothing and serene effect while Gangabal Lake bestows on us peace and tranquility. This is Kashmir, *Kashyapver*, the wonderland of the Himalayas.

*Excerpts from Dr. R.K. Taimiri, Shri Suraj Tickoo, Nilamat Purana, Rajatarangini and the book: Kashmir History and People.*

□

# Vijay Vihar and Kah Kah Pal

The mysticism of the sacred geography of Kashmir has not been hidden from anyone and it is important we keep telling our children about these places and their corresponding spiritual power. We feel these will galvanise them and consequently rekindle inquisitiveness amongst them for *Maej Kasheer.*

Amongst many places, one such place that comes to our minds is Vejibror, the ancient Vijeshwar or Vijay Vihar located on the left bank of the Vitasta River. It is an ancient town mentioned in *Nilamat Purana, Sahitya Prakash, Rajatarangini, Vijayeshwar Mahatamya, Amresh Mahatamya, Vitasta Mahatamya* and *Bhringesh Samhita*. The place and its main shrine is dedicated to the god of victory and is thus known as Vijayeshwara. According to the *Vijayeshwar Mahatmya*:

Earth is the essence of the universe,

The Himalayas occupy the place of pride on the earth, Kashmir is of greater importance than the Himalayas,

But sacred *tirth* of Vijeshwara is of far greater importance. This sacred town was an ancient seat of learning where a university on the pattern of Nalanda and Taxila was established by the Kashmiri thinkers, scholars, and philosophers. During the golden age of knowledge in Kashmir from the 8th to 13th century, many scholars learnt, worked and taught here. Pandit Kalhana completed the history of Kashmir known as *Rajatarangini* at this place. Kshemaraja wrote *Shaiva-Siddhanta*, Acharya Somadeva wrote *Kathasaritsagara*and *Baital Pachisi* at Vijeshwara.

Kalhana in *Rajatarangini* deals with the history and religious importance of the town extensively.

According to him, Raja Vijay Anand was responsible for building the magnificent town and the magnificent temple dedicated to Lord Shiva. Around the temple rose the outstanding university, the great centre of learning that taught subjects such as logic, reasoning, crystal gazing, star gazing, writing, pharmaceuticals, Hindu and Buddhist sacred texts, structural engineering, figure painting, music, grammar, philosophy and astrology etc. The scholars came from Afghanistan, China and the rest of India.

The magnificent Shiva temple was one of the best examples of Kashmiri temple architecture and sculpture. It is said that the temple was so grand and towers so lofty that its shadow fell on Martand Temple 10 kilometres away. The great temple and the university were destroyed in the 14th century by fanatic Muslim rulers. The temple was devastated; the library and manuscripts burnt, the teachers, monks and scholars were killed.

The statues of gods and goddesses strewn on different *ghats* of Vitasta and around show the pinnacle of art and architecture this town had achieved. Many of these sculptures are now with the archaeological survey of India and stand as testimony to the glory of the town. Besides these sources, folk songs and folk tales give us an insight into the rich culture and civilisation of the place.

## Vijay Vihar—A Great Centre of Astrology

The ancient school of astrology, the Vijeshwar Karyalaya developed in Vijay Vihar. Astrology was one of the important subjects taught in the university. Even with the destruction of the university, some of the exponents saved the books and manuscripts and went into hiding. Much later, they returned to the village to pursue their traditional vocation. People from all over India came to consult them till 1990. Unfortunately, the main street, which was inhabited by astrologers, is devoid of them today. All of them moved to Jammu after terrorists killed one of the Hindu residents publically in broad daylight. Fortunately, the doyen of astrology, Pandit Prem Nath Shastri set up Vijeshwar Karyalaya in Jammu to preserve the ancient astrological wisdom and knowledge. His son Omkar Nath Shastri is now carrying on the great astrological tradition of Kashmir.

## Kah Kah Pal

One of the attractive features of this place used to be 'Kah Kah Pal' installed here by a great ancient saint, Shivet Pandit. 'Kah Kah Pal' means the ' Eleven Eleven Stone'. It is a wonder stone found in the garden of the Shiva temple. This conch shaped stone, tapering at one end, weighs about 60 kg and can be moved from side to side by one adult but cannot be lifted. The magic about the stone is that if eleven people encircle it and merely touched its base with their eleven index fingers and chant Kah-Kah (eleven-eleven), the stone gets lifted several feet above the ground. This has been experienced by many locals, and people visiting from outside. It is believed that once the stone was thrown away into the river because of these magical powers but the stone reappeared the next day on the river bank.

Whenever we went from Srinagar to Anantnag, the bus driver would stop the bus at Vejibror and he would shout Kah

Kah Pal-Kah Kah Pal. We would all get down from the bus and rush to have a go at the magic stone. Many times, we have joined the arc of strangers encircling the stone and lifted it. The thrill, awe and mystery created by this act are unforgettable.

However, it is reported that this miraculous oval-shaped stone has been stolen and is missing since militancy and efforts are on to trace it.

□

# Gift of Goddesses Vitasta and other Rivers of Kashmir in Nilamata Purana

Vitasta, the scared river of Kashmir is revered as a divine gift. According to canto 237–238 of Nilamat Purana, Sage Kashyapa seeing the valley so nicely settled with people prayed to Lord Shiva for requesting Devi Uma to give the gift of water to Kashmir Valley. Goddess Uma herself came here in the form of the Vitasta River, the destroyer of the sins.

Not only Uma, but various other goddesses also made Kashmir their home by taking the form of sacred rivers. Sage Kashyapa motivated Vishnu to urge Goddess Lakshmi to purify the land of Kashmir in the form of the Vishoka River. According to canto 249–250, Kashyapa motivated other goddesses by saying that I have created a beautiful place called Kashmir. You goddesses with a pleasant smile give the gift of your sacred waters to honour this land. Thus the mother of gods Aditi came down as Trikuta River.

The wife of Indra, Suchi came down as Harshapatha. Diti came down as Chandravati River and the Yamuna gave a part of itself to Vitasta.

The canto 246–247 says that Shiva's most noble consort Sati appeared as Kashmira Devi. Kashmir should be considered the body part of Shiva and Shiva should be always obeyed.

## Vitasta Mahatmya

The glory of River Vitasta is mentioned in *Nilamata Purana* in cantos 1424 to 1453. It is believed that if one listens to the glory of the sacred river Vitasta, one will be liberated from all the sins. Hence, Janamejaya requests Vaisampayana to narrate the same to him. In canto 1423 of *Nilamata Purana*, Janamejaya asks Vaisampayana, "O best among the twice-born, tell me again the glorification of the Vitasta. I shall become free from all sins by listening to that. Vaisampayana explains that Vitasta was none other than the beautiful Sati, the daughter of Daksha and the beloved wife of Hara (Shiva), who was also known as Uma in *Vaivasvata Antara*.

The one who bathes in Vitasta gets relieved of all sins and feels relieved of all burdens.

The same daughter of the *Himadri* was the sin-destroying Yamuna and the same was spoken of as the greatest boat in the three worlds, to ferry humans across the *samsara* at the end of *Manvantara.*

The same goddess is called Kasmira and the same is the river Vitasta.

The river goddess arose from the Nether World with the stroke of the spear.

On account of bathing in her waters, one realises enlightenment.

Vaisampayana further says that the Ganga does not excel the Vitasta. The only thing which the water of the Ganga has more than that of the Vitasta is the heap of the bones of men. Bath and other things are equal.

He says that Ganga was brought down formerly by King Bhagiratha desirous of deluging the bones of the high-minded Sagaras, so she is stated to be famous in that act. The auspicious

Vitasta is verily the holy river, remover of all sins.

All those who died with the water of the Vitasta in their bellies, reached heaven like the soma-drinkers.

The gods are satisfied not so much with the sacrifices accompanied by sacrificial fees as they are with those holy waters of the Vitasta.

As our ancestors are satisfied just as with various sorts of offerings of sweet and tasty food, the same way they are satisfied with the offering of just the pure waters of the Vitasta.

The Nagas of various forms, the rivers, the holy places, the gods, the sages, the Gandharvas, the Yakshas and the Rakshasas constantly approach her. The wise should go to her to achieve success.

Varuna, the lord of waters, recognises the man who merely bathes in the Vitasta. How can a man recognised by Varuna fall in hell?

The goddess Vitasta-the destroyer of sins- gives protection with her hand, to the evil-doing sinners falling into hell.

The Vitasta is the staircase to heaven and the giver of the fulfilment of desires. By means of a sky-chariot, it will lead one to Amaravati, containing the swans and the aquatic birds (*Sarasa)*, decorated by the *Cakravakas*, having a colour like that of the sun, garlanded with a network of small bells, swarming with a host of heavenly maidens and resounding with the sounds of the *Vina* and the*Muraja*.

O Chief of the Kings, those men obtain fame on the earth, who go to the goddess Vitasta, endowed with various bridges, decorated with blue and red lotuses, filled with the sounds of the herds of the cows, resounding with the bellowing-sounds, full of fish and tortoises, possessed of good bathing places, giver of the desired objects, possessed of the water which tastes like nectar, charming to the eyes of men and boon-giver like a mother.

O King, pay obeisance to her, the purifying one, praised by the high sages, possessed of tasty water, daughter of the Himalaya who is the king of the mountains, and the wife of Hara in the form of the sea.

The Sindhu, the Trikoti, the Visoka, the holy and auspicious river Harsapatha, the holy Sukha, the Candravati, the Sugandha, the sin-destroying Punyodaka, the Kularani, the sin-removing Krsna, the holy Madhumati and the holy river Parosni go to the boon-giver and celestial Vitasta.

O King, the river Ganga on the matted hair of Sambhu-torn forth by the Moon God and hence called Candrabhaga in the human world, comes to the sacred and extensive Vitasta.

O King, the sacred places, the lakes, the rivers, the tanks, the various types of wells, all these come to the boon-giver Vitasta, on the bright thirteenth of the *Bhadrapada*.

Who can be able, O King, to describe to you the merits of the goddess even in several hundred years? Having heard a little which has been narrated by me with devotion, you should be always devoted to her.

Having listened to the glorification of the Vitasta, one is freed from all sins and having heard the whole of the *Nilamata Purana*, one gets the merit of (the gift of) ten cows.

□

# Yaarbal Vyatha Truvah and Vitasta Poojan

Water is the elixir of life. It is key to human prosperity and had helped wandering tribes settle their roots at a place where there was an abundance of water and fertile land. The air, water and food are the most important elements for human survival and have immensely contributed to the development of civilisations through clústers. While air is all around, food and water are interdependent. For agriculture and food production, we need both fertile land and water. Our rivers not only gave us water for irrigation but also food in the form of fish.

For thousands of years, most civilisations have developed on the banks of the rivers. Whether it was Mohenjodaro on the Indus river in India or the Egyptian civilisation by the river Nile, the Roman civilisation by the river Tiber, Mesopotamia by Euphrates and Tigris, the British by the Thames, northern plains of India by the holy river the Ganges and last but not the least, the valley of Kashmir by our sacred river Vitasta.

In Kashmir valley, the Vitasta River is our lifeline. All our important towns and sacred places are situated on the banks of holy Vitasta or its tributaries. Somnath Sapru in his book *Cashmere-Kashir that was Yarbal,* says that "If you look at the map, you will see population spread not only in Srinagar city proper but other places too like Anantnag, Baramulla, Sopore,

Avantipura, where people have their homes either by the side of the water or near about."

Now the question, how did the word 'yaarbal' came into usage. People give different interpretations of the word yaarbal. The word *yaar-bal* is a compound of two words, yaar and bal. Bal in Kashmiri is used to denote a waterfront location such as Ganga-Bal, Gandher-Bal, Pokhri-Bal etc.

Yaar, on the other hand, is the corruption of 'Vihar' which in Sanskrit means to play or roam around for amusement. Thus vihar bal was the old Kashmiri word for the river bank which meant a pleasant place for strolling, swimming etc. Vihara also means a Buddhist monastery. Many Buddhist Viharas were located on river banks and that could be another reason to call our river banks vihar bal. Hsuan Tsang has mentioned a Buddhist Vihara located at Ganpatyar temple on the river Vitasta where he had stayed for a while.

## Vyatha Truvah and Vitasta Poojan

The yaarbal and Vitasta River has been an integral part of the Kashmiri Pandit culture and the way of life. Yaarbal plays a key role in our spiritual, cultural and religious practices from birth till death. Before 1990, one could hear the sound of temple bells emanating from riverside temples of Ganpatyar, Somayar, the temple of the moon, Porshyar, Batayar, Raghunath Mandir in the mornings and evenings. You could see elderly pandits bathing in the river and doing *Surya Namaskar* and *Sandhya vandanam,* before going to circumambulate Shrine of Goddess Sharika at Hari Parvat. One could see *nirmalayam,* water carrying milk and flowers petals floating on the river, giving it a distinctively sacred character.

Our river Vitasta has been part of our Shivaratri *Vatuk* ceremony, sacred thread ceremony, *Shraddha* ceremony for ancestors and the place for consigning the ashes for our dear departed. For us, it is the holy mother, just like the Ganges. All our important shrines in Srinagar are located on the Vitasta. All its *ghats* are sacred for performing *Surya Namaskar, Sandhyavandanam* to have a holy dip and to offer prayers. It is not surprising, therefore, that we dedicate the 13th day of the bright fortnight of the month of Bhadrapada to the life-giving river Vitasta. On this day, the beloved river is worshipped as the Goddess personified. Just like River Ganges is worshipped in Hardwar and Varanasi and Kaveri is worshipped in Tanjavur so is Vitasta worshipped in Kashmir. It is offered water, milk, vermillion, raw rice and flowers. People also go on a pilgrimage to its source at Vyetha Vottur and Verinag. Today, our yaarbal has been desecrated and encroached upon but the *Shakti* of these spiritual places still exists and will continue to exist. Just like 'Clean Ganga', we have to launch a 'Clean Vitasta' movement.

□

# Part-4

# Scholars, Sages and Kings

# Acharya Abhinavagupta Mystic Scholar or Bhairava

Kashmir is the epicentre of human culture. It has also given the humanity *Pratyabhijna* system of Kashmir Shaivism which is a profound philosophy of life. Indian literature without the contribution of Kashmir would be hollow. Kashmir has produced numerous scholars such as Vamana, the founder of the Riti School, Udbhatta, the teacher of different theories of Riti, Ananda Vardhana, the founder of Dhvani School, Mammatta the founder of Rasa School, in addition to Kayyatta, Ruyyaka, Rudratta, and Mahima Batta. Patanjali also produced much of his work while in Kashmir. Kashmir not only contributed to poetics and literature, but also created many philosophers and mystics.

Among them, an important philosopher Attrigupta was brought to Kashmir by King Lalitaditya from Kannauj after he conquered North India. Attrigupta's distinguished descendants included Narasimha Gupta and his son Abhinavagupta. Acharya Abhinavagupta enriched India's philosophical traditions in a way that has not been replicated since.

He was one of India's greatest philosophers, mystics and aestheticians and also an outstanding musician, poet, dramatist, theologian, and logician. He was a polymathic personality who exercised strong influences on Indian culture. He studied under at least 15 teachers and in his long life, completed over 41 works. The largest and most famous of which is 'Tantrāloka', an encyclopaedic treatise on all the philosophical and practical aspects of *Trika* and *Kaula* philosophy of Kashmir Shaivism.

Abhinavagupta's *Tantraloka* and *Pratyabhijna Virmarshini* though acclaimed to be the mere expositions of the *Pratyabhijna Sutra* of Utpal Deva are original works of high merit. According to Dr. B.N. Pandit, Kashmir Shaivism is the only philosophy that can inspire human beings both for material as well as spiritual advancement. Thus Abhinavagupta's contribution to Shaivite philosophy is unique and enormous. He rose to the position of *Acharya* and is considered the greatest exegetical theologian of the Shaiva tradition in the medieval period.

## Tantraloka

*Tantraloka* was written around the 11th century. After Kashmir Shaivism all but disappeared, it was rediscovered among the old manuscripts towards the end of the 19th century. It was translated into Italian by Raniero Gnoli. John Dupuche translated its 29th chapter containing 'Kaula Rituals' in English. There was no authentic full translation in English available in the recent past. The last living master of the Oral Tradition of Kashmir Shaivism, Swami Lakshmanjoo, gave a condensed version of key philosophical chapters of *Tantraloka* in his book, 'Kashmir Shaivism-The Secret Supreme'.

*Tantraloka* or 'Light on the Tantras' is one of the great accomplishments in Indian theology. It appears to have been committed to writing after Abhinavagupta had attained nirvana. It weaves together citations from dozens of authoritative scriptures, into a monumental 12-volume encyclopaedic work. The many quotations in the *Tantraloka* appear to have been cited from memory. Its discourse moves among the realms of rigorous logical philosophy, scripturally-grounded theology, and personal mystical experience. It influenced theological thought and the understanding of the inner meaning of ritual in the Shaiva and Shakta schools for many centuries to come.

Abhinavagupta's creation is well-balanced between the branches of the triad (*Trika*), will (*icchā*), knowledge (*jñāna*) and action (*kriyā*). The essence of the entire teaching is that whatever we do for our spiritual development is ultimately to achieve the recognition that there is only that one reality and it is 'who we are: we are that Lord Shiva' who is shining and manifesting as all things.

In the words of Dr. Mark Dyczkowski, one of the world's foremost scholars on 'Tantra and Kashmiri Shaivism', "Kashmir Shaivism explains that reality is understood to be just one, and that reality is Lord Shiva. He is the pure conscious nature that manifests as all things. Like a light that shines and illumines everything, the light of consciousness shines, illuminating its infinite manifestations. This shining of Lord Shiva is eternal, unending, undivided, and in all ways unconditioned. What we live and experience in our daily lives, in every moment, is part of that immense consciousness. He shines, manifests, and is everything and everybody—all that happens in our lives, as well as how we perceive it all."

While tantrism is a complex and controversial subject, one of its most definitive characteristics for contemporary classifications—if not its most definitive one—is the pursuit of power. Tantric traditions are thus those that aim at increasing the power of the practitioner. In Shākta tantrism, Shakti as a Goddess is herself the ultimate deity. In monistic Kashmiri Shaivism, she is incorporated into the metaphysical essence of the God Shiva. Shiva is the 'Shaktiman' (the 'possessor of Shakti') encompassing her within his androgynous nature as his integral power and consort.

Explaining Acharya Abhinavagupta is not easy. For some, he remains a polymath, a philosopher, a commentator, a rational monist, a great mystic and for others, he is a Bhairava, the Shiva incarnate.

Swami Ramji Maharaj, the great mystic of mid 19th century Kashmir said, "Wash your hands and feet, rinse your mouth well and then if you recite the name of 'Abhinavagupta' you shall attain *Moksha*." To Swami Ramji, the name of Abhinavagupta was like a phenomenal mantra which if recited with a clean and pure mind had the power of liberating a person.

'Abhinavagupta' was not his real name, rather a title he earned from his teachers, meaning competence and authoritativeness. Italian Shaivite scholar Raniero Gnoli mentions that 'Abhinava' also means 'new' as a reference to the ever-new creative force of his mystical experience.

Later writers have referred to him as 'Abhinavaguptapada.' The word *pada* is an honorific, but it also means 'serpent Shesa Naga'. 'Abhinavaguptapada' would thus mean 'a new incarnation of Shesha', the serpent God, one of the manifestations of Vishnu.

Vamana, the propounded of 'Riti' school in Indian rhetoric and commentator of 'Kavya Prakasha' known as 'Bala Bodhini' has alluded to *Abhinavaguptapada* as an intellectual giant and like a serpent creating awe among scholars, colleagues and disciples.

Abhinavagupta's other outstanding contributions was in the field of aesthetics with his famous *Abhinavabhāratī* which is a rare commentary of *Nāṭyaśāstra* of Bharata Muni, which is the base of all classical dances of India including Bharat Natyam, Kathak, Odissi, Kuchipudi, Kathakali, Manipuri and so on. When the dance is all but wiped out from Kashmir, we need to remember the greatest work on *Nāṭyaśāstra* was produced in Kashmir by Acharya Abhinavagupta. The earliest mention of dance being performed according to *Nāṭyaśāstra* also comes from the Sun Temple of Martand in Kashmir. His doctrine on *Rasadhvani* is considered to be the very soul of literature.

The world, specifically the European scholars have taken a keen interest in knowing and exploring him. His commentaries on Anandavardhana's *Dhvanyaloka* and Bharat Muni's *Nāṭyaśāstra* made him famous all over the country even during his lifetime. His brush with the western world came when in the middle part of the 19th century, they started pouring into the valley of Kashmir. H.H. Buhler, M.A. Stein and others led the research. Many more scholars of fame Dr. Kaviraaj Gopinaath, Dr. K.C. Pandey, Navjeevan Rastogi, Dr. V. Raghavan, Prof. M.L. Pandit, Dr. B.N. Pandit, S.C. Banerji, K. Krishnamoorthy, G.V. Tagree, Andre Padoux, J.L. Masson, M.V. Patvardhan, Edwin Gerow, Gerald James Lawson, Donna Wolf, K.D. Tripathi, Sir John Woodroffe, Ingalls, Natalia Mikhailova, Raniero Gnoli, Lilian Silburn, Boris Marjanovic, Jai Dev Singh, John R. Dupche, Paul Eduardo Muller, Paul E. Murphey, Alexis G. Sanderson, Betina Baumer, Mark Dyzcowiski, Singo Einoo, Gabriel Pradipika, Jurgen Hanneder researched his works and were fascinated by the irresistible charm of Acharya Abhinavagupta.

According to local tradition, his Gurukul had 12,000 students. When he felt the mission of this life was completed, he chose the time and place of his departure. Followed by his 12000 students, chanting, 'Bhairav Sutra', he walked into Bhairava cave at Magam, between Srinagar and Gulmarg and was never seen again. This cave is called *Batte Goph.* It is said that he went into the void and merged with Shiva.

This year, we completed the millennial year of Acharya Abhinavagupta and the nation needs to commemorate this. This is a real pride moment for India and the Kashmiri Pandits in particular. It is also a reminder to us to follow his teachings and recognise ourselves as part of 'one' reality and know who we are.

*Excerpts & References from Dr. Mark Dyczkowski, David Peter Lawrence, Shri Jawahar Lal Ganhar, Dr. Krishna Raina, Shri Pradeep Khali.*

□

# Adi Shankracharya and Shakti Cult of Kashmir

Kashmir is known for its Shakti cult, the female-oriented system. Nowhere else in the world one can see a religious system where Shakti is considered as an important source of creation and realisation. This is one of the unique and fundamental tenets of 'Shaktism.'

It is believed that Adi Shankara, till he came to Kashmir was not familiar with the greatness of Shakti. It was during his stay in Kashmir that he had many close encounters with Shakti in different forms and eventually became an ardent devotee of Devi.

Before encountering the glory of Shakti, Shankara was always keen to engage in a debate with the followers of the Shakti Cult. Once, when he wanted to challenge their views, he became a victim of a prolonged illness. His illness made him weak and crippled his strength. He was neither able to take a single step nor able to utter a single word. His body had completely given up when a small girl appeared before him. She questioned him, how he intended to challenge the disciples of Shakti for a debate in this state. Adi Shankara helplessly replied that his illness had made him too weak to debate but as soon as he recovered from the illness and regained some 'Shakti', he would go for the debate.

The girl again enquired, "When you cannot move an inch

without your Shakti, how will you refute the cult of Shakti?" She further added, "O Wise One, know me to be Shiva's Shakti—The supreme power activating this world. Charged by my own energy, you want to negate me?" He recognised Goddess Sharada in the little girl and bowed to her.

According to P.N. Magzine, a *shastrarth* did take place between Shankara and a Kashmiri Pandit lady which lasted for 17 days after which Shankara yielded and accepted the predominance and the greatness of Devi.

In another story, when Shankracharya was travelling with his disciples, he had to make a halt outside Srinagar city. His hostess, a Pandit lady provided them with all the materials such as food grain, oil, spices, lentils and vegetables and firewood for cooking. It is mentioned that when the lady of the house woke up in the morning, she was surprised to find food uncooked and firewood unlit. On enquiring, she was told that they had nothing with which they could make the fire and so had slept hungry. This amused the Pandit lady, she just sprinkled some drops of water on the firewood and it caught fire.

Another version of the same story says that she picked two pieces of wood, rubbed them against each other while chanting a mantra and the fire was lit. Seeing this phenomenon, Shankara was completely surprised. This further strengthened and deepened his belief in the power of Shakti.

In another legend, Shankara argued that the icon of Devi was a mere representation and not the manifestation of the goddess. Suddenly, the head of the icon started bleeding. The bleeding stopped only when Shankara tore a piece of his garment and tied it around the head of Devi. People say that because of this incident, Kashmiri Pandit women started wearing the traditional 'white band' *Taranga* around their *Kalpush* cap.

After these illuminating incidents, Shankara composed poems in praise of goddess such as *Sharada Bhajana Stotra* and *Soundarya Lahari*. He wrote *Soundarya Lahari* at Gopadari Hill, now known as Shankaracharya Hill. He has mentioned, "If Shiva is united with Shakti, he can create. If he is not, he is incapable even of stirring."

According to Pandit Gopi Krishan, the *Soundaraya Lahari* is the only other work on the theme of Shakti comparable to *Panchastavi*. Shri P.N. Magzine also applauds *Soundarya Lahari* as a masterpiece of Sanskrit literature. In some verses, Shankara refers to the earrings of the Goddess, probably referring to the characteristic long *dejhoor* earrings of Kashmiri women, shaped like an octagonal *yantra* that dangles from the ear.

## Shankara at Sharada Peeth

When Shankara visited Sharada Peeth, Kashmiri scholars were highly appreciative of his knowledge. They accorded him the highest honour when he visited the Shrine of Goddess Sharada and the famous Sharada Peeth University. It is believed that Sharada Peeth had four doors facing the four cardinal directions. The southern door had always remained closed as no southern scholar had come this far to cast his sway. It was open only once in recognition and honour of Adi Shankara after he impressed the resident scholars with his scholarship and decoding of the Vedas. He was made to ascend the throne of *Sarvajnapeetha* 'The Seat of all Wisdom.' Following his visit to Kashmir, Shankara became a staunch believer of Shakti. Shankara Digvijaya mentions that he carried the Sri Chakra, the symbol and vibration of Goddess Sharada from Sharada Peeth to Sringeri Math. He installed the Sri Chakra in Sringeri Math. Hence, Sringeri Math came to be known as Sharada Sringeri Peeth.

These examples strongly indicate how the rich traditions of Kashmiri Pandits have their roots deeply embedded in spiritualism and mysticism and Kashmiri Pandit women are the embodiments of Shakti. Therefore, preservation and practice of our rich culture is critical for our success and glory.

□

# King Lalitaditya of Kashmir

After the last king of the Gonanda Dynasty died, DurlabhVardhana of the Karkota Dynasty took over. Lalitaditya was the youngest grandson of DurlabhVardhana. He came to the throne after his brother Chandrapida and Tarapida ruled for eight years and four years respectively. He was the 5th King of the Karkota (Naga) Dynasty and ruled for almost 37 years from 695 to 732 AD.

Kalhana, the brilliant historian, in the 4th Taranga of *Rajatarangini* describes the adventures of Lalitaditya of Kashmir. He further says about Lalitaditya, "The king, who carried his prowess, abandoned his (war-like) fury (only) when the (opposing) kings discreetely folded their palms at his victorious onset. At the sound of his drums (beaten) in attack, the dwellings of his enemies were diverted by the (frightened) inhabitants." *Rajatarangini* repeatedly mentions his conquests over Jalamdhara (Jalandhar), Lohara (Loren near Poonch), Kannauj,

Kambhoj (eastern Afghanistan), Vindhyas, Karnat (Karnatka) and Konkan region. Besides Kalhana, the Chinese, Turkish and Tibetan legends also refer to him as a great conqueror.

Kalhana described Lalitaditya as a very strong ruler who asserted his power far beyond Kashmir and adjacent territories. He was a great conqueror whose reign was mostly spent in expeditions. For his numerous foreign expeditions and his ultimate disappearance during one of these forays towards the north, many scholars have compared him with the Greek conqueror, Alexander the Great. They both had similar dispositions and thus he is called Lalitaditya, the Alexander of Kashmir.

He had one of the biggest empires in the world, bigger than Mauryan and Mughal empires. At its peak, it is mentioned to be 8 million square miles in area, much more than what Alexander had conquered. It extended from Tibet to Iran and Turkistan. He ruled Persia, defeated Arabs and halted their expansion into Indus Valley. He also conquered a large part of India and was also known as the Monarch of India.

According to one theory, many communities in Kerala are supposed to be the progeny of settlers from different parts of Asia, especially from Kashmir who arrived during King Lalitaditya's time. Namboodiris and Nairs are believed to be from Kashmir. The Nairs in Kerala are 'Naga' worshippers which somewhat relates to the Naga practices of Kashmir.

Aberuni, a medieval traveller mentions that Kashmiris of his time used to celebrate an annual festival on the second day of the holy month of Chaitra, the day following Navreh, the Kashmiri New Year, to commemorate the victory of King Lalitaditya Muktapida on Turks.

Lalitaditya is generally accepted as the most powerful king of his dynasty. He commissioned several shrines in Kashmir, including the grand temple of Martand in honour of the Sun deity Bhaskar. This great specimen of architecture was destroyed by Sultan Sikandar Butshikan in 14th century.

Though Lalitaditya was Hindu by faith, he showed great

respect for Buddhism and built numerous Buddhist shrines and viharas. He was a great builder and established several towns and built a new capital at Parihaspura. He remains one of the outstanding kings of Kashmir and India.

To sum up in the words of Shri Shashi Shekhar Toshkhani, noted Poet, writer and scholar from Kashmir, "Lalitaditya was not only a great conqueror but also an equally great patron of the arts. It was during his time that Kashmir evolved an indigenous style of temple architecture marked for its grandeur. We cannot forget that it was Lalitaditya who promoted Shaivite scholarship and brought Great Shaiva scholar Attrigupta from Antarvedi in modern Uttar Pradesh to live and teach in Kashmir. Many generations later, Attrigupta's descendent Abhinavagupta, emerged as the greatest Shaivite scholar of Kashmir and revived the Kashmir Shaivism.

□

# King Avantivarman

## And his Prime Minister Suyya

The history of Kashmir Pandit is full of gems such as warriors, reformers, philosophers, poets, architects, artists, spiritual gurus and able administrators. Among the galaxy of such names, Kashmir has also had a talented ruler in Avantivarman – who ruled between 855-883 CE. He is known for his constructive and consolidating efforts rather than for his conquests. The town of Avantipura which is named after him survives to this day.

Avantivarman belonged to Utpala Dynasty and was the grandson of Utpala, the founder of the dynasty. He is considered one of the most outstanding Kashmiri Kings, who built cities, temples and infrastructure. After 40 years of civil war, when he came to the throne, he restored peace and prosperity in the valley. The remarkable achievement of his reign was the execution of a flood prevention scheme in the valley to drain away the excess rainwater. It was an engineering feat executed with the help of Suyya. Avantivarman had appointed a great and intelligent Kashmiri engineer Suyya as his prime minister. More than thousand years ago, Suyya diagnosed correctly that the floods in the valley were because the rapid waters of the Jhelum River were not able to get through the narrow gorge three miles below *Varahmula.* In addition, this constricted passage often got blocked with boulders. Suyya desilted the

Vitasta River after removing the boulders and also changed the course of the river to channelise the excess water for irrigation and cultivation.

Suyya adopted a novel method to have the boulders removed from the river. On Avantivarman's orders, he threw gold and silver coins into the river where the obstructing boulders lay. Soon word spread that there was money at the bottom of the river and men dashed in to retrieve it. They rooted up all the obstructing boulders in their search for money and paved the way for desilting the river. As a result of the removal of the obstruction and regulation of the course of the Vitasta, periodically devastating floods, as well as consequent famines, were arrested. In addition, a large tract of land also became available for cultivation. The water was channelised for irrigation, which boosted the agricultural operations. This increased paddy production, leading to the decline of paddy prices and making food available to the common man at a cheaper price. Thus, besides saving the local masses from frequent floods, he made earnest efforts to ameliorate the economic condition of the people.

Apart from Avantipura, Suyyapura, present Sopore town in Baramulla district of Kashmir was also founded by Avantivarman with the help of Suyya.

King Avantivarman made himself illustrious by virtue of his peaceful pursuits, conscientious care of his subjects and liberal patronage of arts and learning. He did not launch on an ambitious career of conquests. His just and peaceful rule of 28 years was further made memorable by a large number of religious foundations and endowments, not only by himself but by his relatives and officials.

Avantivarman erected two magnificent temples, one dedicated to Lord Vishnu called 'Avantisvamin' and the other to Lord Shiva called 'Avantisvara'. He was a devout worshipper of Lord Vishnu from his childhood and remained a Vaishnavite at the core of his heart till his death. The similarity to these temples with the Sun Temple in Martand is striking. Both the

Sun Temple and the temples in Avantipura show an outward influence of Greek architecture. It is not clear whether it is Greek architecture or Greeks imported it from Kashmir.

Avantivarman encouraged scholarship and his reign witnessed a remarkable revival of Sanskrit learning in Kashmir. His court was adorned by men of learning and poets such as Muktakana, Anandavardhana the author of Dhvanyaloka, Kalatta, the great pupil of Vasu Gupta and the founder of *Spanda Shastra* division of Kashmir Shaivism and Ratnakara who wrote *Haravijaya*. However, the greatest scholar of his time was Swamivarmin.

Avantivarman is one king Kashmiris can be proud of. □

# Utpaladeva—Am I Shiva? The Power of Consciousness

Utpaladeva, son of Udayakara, a well-known scholar was born around 900 CE. From his childhood, he was a precocious child with a sharp intellect and quest for knowledge. He grew to become the great Kashmiri mystic and the teacher of Kashmir Shaivism. It is he who said Lord Shiva and You are one in the consciousness. A great writer and devotional poet, through his hymns he proclaimed:

"This is also a great wonder to me that in reality, by nature, this mind is the seed of pain, sorrow, sadness and torture. But this seed, when watered with the nectar of devotion to Thee, bears the fruit of final liberation."

These hymns he wrote are known as 'Shivastotravali' or the Hymns to Shiva. Although these were composed more than a thousand years ago, they are still recited by devotees every day. The 'Hymns to Shiva' is probably the greatest example of Kashmiri Shaivite devotional poetry. These captivating verses were born in the valley of Kashmir around picturesque Dal Lake as an inspirational outpouring of devotion from the heart of the spiritual master.

These hymns are so profound that they have the power to free the devotee from the restrictions of their intellect and instantaneously elevate them to the experience of oneness with the very nature of their divine consciousness. Through these, Utpaladeva taught us that devotion or the 'passion for Godconsciousness' is all that matters.

Another of his illustrious work 'Ishwara-Pratyabhijna-Karikas' contain the verses on the 'Recognition of the Lord'. With his sharp intellect, he re-established the philosophy of 'recognition' of oneself or 'self-cognition'. This doctrine of Utpaladeva can be understood with the following example:

A girl and a boy, whose marriage has been fixed by their relatives but have not seen each other, happen to sit together along with their friends and relatives at a fair. The girl and boy have no special feelings for each other. But when the girl serves the refreshments to the boy and an acquaintance hints at their pending marriage, the feelings of love rush through the mind and the heart of the boy and the girl. The girl recognises her lover. Such is the recognition of Jiva with Shiva. This is Pratyabhijna philosophy in a nutshell, as preached comprehensively by Utpala. He sat and wrote these abstruse aphorisms on the philosophy in calm moments of self-introspection.

Utpaladeva rejects the notion of a mind-independent realm of particulars. He thinks that the experience of a structured reality requires that both subjects and objects belong to a single field of experience. According to his theory, the cosmos is manifested by a single, transcendental conscious dynamism. Categories such as individual substance, action, relation, nature, quality, space, time and the cause-effect relation are objective realities because they are manifestations projected by the transcendental consciousness. Through its innate powers of unregulated will, vast knowledge and action, the supreme creates all subjects, objects and occasions of experience in a structured framework of time and space. The dynamic and utterly independent Lord Shiva's consciousness is modelled on one's experience of consciousness which oscillates between the illumination of objectivity and reflective awareness. This is influenced by the grammarian Bhartrihari's principle that without linguistic expression, there can be no awareness. Utpaladeva emphasises the liberty of individual subjective awareness which is inspired by the compelling visions produced in meditation.

The mystic Utpaladeva was a loving and pure-hearted soul who influenced any number of future saints and sages of Kashmir such as Lalleshwari, Nund Rishi, Rupa Bhawani and Swami Rama Tirtha. His poems give a devotional expression to the philosophical doctrines of Kashmir Shaivism known as the 'Trika'. These are as important in Kashmir Shaivism as the Vedanta Stotras are in Vedanta philosophy.

Utpaladeva's philosophy is as deep as that of Adi Shankaracharya. It is characterised by a unique blend of metaphysics, epistemology, linguistic philosophy and religious experience. Utpaladeva through his arguments led his students to the recognition of their identity with Lord Shiva. Kashmir's Persian scholars have termed it as Khird-e-Kamil—the wisdom of the sage.

We must revisit the *Shivastrotavali*-'Hymns to Shiva' of Utpaladeva and revive the fading concepts, where lies the real power and strength and ammunition for our resurgence.

Given below are a few verses from *Shivastotravali*.

1. Only those who are immersed
   In the joy of fervent devotion
   Know the essence of the Lord
   Of your boundless ocean of bliss.
2. You alone, O Lord, are the self of all.
   And everyone naturally loves his own self.
   Thus victorious becomes the one who knows
   That devotion is inherent in all.
3. Lord! when the objective world is dissolved
   Through a state of deep meditation

And who does not see you then?
But even in the state of differentiation
   Between the knower and the known,
   You are easily seen by the devotees.

4. Just as Devi,
 Your most beloved, endless pool of bliss,
 Is inseparable from you,
 So may your devotion alone
 Be inseparable from me.

*Excerpts from Swami Lakshmanjoo's publications, Kashmir Shaivism and India Religion write-ups.*

□

# Swami Vivekananda—The Mystical Experiences of Kashmir that Shook his Mind

The first visit of Swami Vivekananda to Kashmir was brief but the spiritual power of this place touched him so deeply that he was attracted to come back in mid of June 1898 again. On 3rd July when Bhagwan Gopinath was born, Swami Vivekananda appeared suddenly at his Safa Kadal residence and blessed the newborn baby.

During this visit, he was accompanied by his European friends and travelled to many religious and historical places such as Shri Amarnath, Mata Kheer Bhawani, Sun temple of Martand etc.

The pilgrimage to Martand got revived due to Swami Vivekananda. On the way to Amarnath, Swami went searching for the site of the ancient Sun temple which had remained abandoned since its destruction by Sikandar Butshikan in the 14th century. Only seven shepherd families lived in the village. The visit of Swami brought the ancient forgotten village into the limelight and many pilgrims started visiting the village. As a result, some Pandits from Sopore and Khrew, where the holy shrine of Goddess Jwala Ji exists, came to Martand to attend to the visiting pilgrims and settled there permanently. This revived the rituals for the deceased and conducting of the ancestral worship over here. The small community of these Pandits has grown into the present-day Pandas and Purohits of Martand. After the displacement, the Pandas of Martand moved to Jammu where they have constructed a temple dedicated to the Sun God.

Swami Vivekananda had a great fascination for Lord Shiva since his childhood. As he grew older, his love for Shiva, the God of monks and yogis deepened. At Kashmir, amid the Himalayas, the abode of Shiva, the thoughts of Shiva were uppermost in his mind.

When he first entered the shrine of Amarnath, he was nude except for his loin-cloth and prostrated before the ice-lingam. His experience was exalting. He said, "I thought the ice-lingam was Shiva Himself." He told Sister Nivedita that Lord Shiva appeared before him and granted him his grace.

Following the pilgrimage to Amarnath, his love for the Divine Mother also grew intense. At Srinagar, he worshipped the four-year daughter of his Muslim boatman as Goddess Uma.

## Turning Point

Later, Swami Vivekananda left for Tul Mul to visit the temple of Mata Kheer Bhawani. He left strict instructions to his party not to follow him. He stayed there alone for a week and practised severe austerities. Each day, he performed a *havan* and offered *kheer* to the Mother Goddess. Every morning, he worshipped a Brahmin Pandit's little daughter as a form of Goddess Uma.

In the presence of the divine Mother, he became like a small child. All thoughts of his role as a spiritual leader, worker, or teacher vanished from his mind and he was now only a mere monk, in all nakedness of pure *Sannyasa.*

One day at Kheer Bhawani, he had been pondering over the ruination and desecration of the temple by the Muslim invaders. Distressed at heart, he thought: "How could the people have permitted such sacrilege without offering strenuous resistance! If I had been here then, I would never have allowed such a thing. I would have laid down my life to protect the Mother. Thereupon, he heard the voice of the Goddess saying:

I desired that the Muslims destroy the temple. It is my desire that I should live in a dilapidated temple, otherwise, can I not immediately erect a seven-story temple of gold here if I like? What can you do? Do I protect you or do you protect me?

Referring to this incident, Swami exclaimed, "All my patriotism is gone, everything is gone. Now it is only Mother! Mother! Mother! I have been very wrong. I am only a little child."

*Swami Vivekananda in Kashmir*

The visions he had at these places had a significant impact on him and changed his entire spiritual experience.

Yet another anecdote says that at Tul Mul, he picked up a Muslim devotee, a man he had cured of migraine by placing his hand over the head.

This man used to be a devotee of a local fakir. The fakir on losing a disciple, in anger, cursed the man in 'ochre robes' saying, "Before you leave this valley, you shall taste your blood. You shall remember, you too have a body. You shall vomit blood. Mark my words!" And these words soon came true. The story goes: Just before leaving the valley, Vivekananda vomited blood. It shook his core. Once back at Belur Math, Sharada Ma, the wife of Shri Ramakrishna told him, 'Even Shankaracharya couldn't survive these machinations'.

Thus we see during his stay in Kashmir, Swami Vivekananda was in a different world altogether. Visions of Shri Amarnath, Mother Kali and Kheer Bhawani always remained with him. Later at Belur Math, he said, "Since visiting Amarnath, I feel as though Shiva is sitting on my head twenty-four hours a day and will not come down"

It is often said that the vision at Tul Mul made him realise who he is and what purpose he has to fulfil in this world. His Guru, Ramakrishna Paramahamsa had once prophesied to his close disciples that when Vivekananda realises who he is, he will not like to live anymore and would depart from this world. On 4 July, 1902, Swami Vivekananda at the age of 39 years, departed from this world fulfilling his own prophecy that "I shall not live to be forty years old."

*Excerpts from Swami Bodhasarananda's compilations on Vivekananda's experience in Kashmir and writing of Prof. R.K. Pandit.*

□

# Bhagwan Gopinathji

## Jagat Guru who Continues to Lead us from Darkness to Light

It is not uncommon in Kashmir that a sage is born in an ordinary household. There is a saying in Kashmiri "*Lembi manz pamposh phatan*" meaning lotus grows in mud. Kashmir has been blessed to give birth to saints like Bhagwan Gopinathji. He was a great mystic and a *jeevanmukta* of Kashmir and the only one to be addressed as Bhagwan by his disciples.

His spiritual state has been described as *Shambhavi* state, a state of Shiva consciousness. He was also called *Aghoreshwara*-the lord of the cremation ground. During his lifetime, he was declared a *Jagat Guru and a*fter his *nirvana*, he was placed in Kreem Kund in Varanasi amid a galaxy of *aghoreshwaras* by Swami Ram.

He was born on 3rd July 1898 in Bana Mohalla, Srinagar to Pandit Narayan Joo Bhan and Shrimati Harmali. There is an amazing story connected with his birth. Around that time, Swami Vivekananda was on a pilgrimage to Kashmir. Out of the blue, he paid a visit to the Bhan family on the occasion of the birth of Bhagwan and blessed the newborn.

His mother died leaving several children when he was only twelve. He completed his school education at Tyndale Biscoe Memorial School in Fateh Kadal where he studied Sanskrit, Persian, and Urdu.

Since his childhood, he only wanted to engage in spiritual pursuits and was very reluctant to take up any bread-winning employment. However, due to his family circumstances, he was forced to start work early in life.

After initially assisting his maternal uncle in his 'pashmina wool' business, he worked as a compositor at the Vishi Nath Press in Srinagar. For the next ten years, he ran grocery stores at Sekidafar and Chaayidob. At the shop, he was always in and out of his meditative state. Despite all the pressure from his family, he refused to marry.

From the age of twenty-two, he circumambulated Hari Parvat every day. He was found in the temple courtyard meditating or smoking his *chillum.* At the age of twenty-seven, he had a vision of Goddess Sharika at Hari Parvat which led to his abandoning the material world to take up the full-time spiritual practice.

After he had given up running the shop, he plunged headlong into rigorous spiritual discipline, staking his very life with an iron will and a remarkable determination.

He attended *satsang* of saints and scholars and was deeply involved in the study of Vedanta and Kashmir Shaivism. He stressed that knowledge does not come by merely reading and memorising like a parrot but by perception, vision and yoga. He said that the experienced truth is supreme and superior to that acquired by reading and listening.

It is surmised that Swami Zankak was his Guru and Swami Aftab Joo Wangnoo his *gurubhai.* He always kept a copy of Bhagawad Gita by his side. A few years before his death, when a devotee enquired about his guru, Bhagwan Ji pointed towards Bhagawad Gita and said any of its 7000 verses can be considered his spiritual gurus.

Bhagawad Gita says, *"Anekajanmasansiddhahtato yati param-gatim"* A seeker gets perfected over several births and then only attains the exalted spiritual position". The exalted spiritual position that Bhagwan Ji attained during his lifetime stands testimony to the fact that he had many highly successful spiritual past lives, the cumulative effect of which enabled him to merge with the divine during his present life.

Every morning, after washing his face and *Yajnopavit* - sacred thread, he would sit on his asana. He would put on his turban and apply a *tilak* of saffron and a little ash on his forehead. Thereafter, he would light his *dhooni* in an iron *sigdi* and perform a *satvik yajna* by offering sugar, rice, barley, nuts, mint and skimmia leaves.

He was particular that the *dhooni* should always be in flame. For him, it was not a mere act of burning charcoal. He gave great importance to the light *Prakasha* represented by the flame which resonates with the Vedic hymn, "Tamsaso Ma Jyotirgamaya"- lead me from the darkness to light.

Slowly, he moved from *Saguna-Upasana* to *Nirguna-Upasana*, meditating on formless God. His most arduous *sadhana* was between 1930 and 1937 when he was totally absorbed in the spiritual world while lying on a cot with his face to the wall. For seven years, he isolated himself in a dark room where just an oil lamp burned continuously.

He undertook extreme penance involving self-abnegation and fasting. Sometimes he fasted for months. His room and bed were covered with dust and cobwebs and spiders but he would not let anyone in to clean the place. A rat is said to have nibbled a hole into his heels while he remained unaware of the pain. His body became swollen and he vomited blood. During this time, he practiced Tantra Yoga. He emerged from this *sadhana* as an omniscient yogi, who had seen Shiva face to face and became a *Sidha Purusha,* the one with spiritual powers or *Siddhis.*

It is authentically known that he had good command over Persian, Sanskrit and Urdu and on Devanagari and Sharda scripts. Many devotees have vouched that in his ecstatic mood, he uttered beautiful sentences in English as well. It is also said that when the 'Kashmir' issue was being debated in the UN Security Council, he had uttered a few sentences in an unintelligible language, which turned out to be Russian. Eventually, these very sentences were spoken by the Russian delegate the next day while vetoing the anti-India resolution of the UN Security Council backed by Western powers.

He was indifferent to everything external. In the matter of food, he used to say that one should not eat when one is hungry but feed his body only when there is no urge for eating. This was obviously to conquer hunger and thirst as he would go without food for days together and sometimes eat ravenously.

Many miracles are ascribed to him. He delayed the death of a person till the wedding of his daughter was solemnised. He cured many patients from severe ailments. He rescued many of his devotees from imminent dangers. Above all, he enabled a fortunate few to have a glimpse of the Mother Goddess in the form of a small girl, whom he fed savouries with his own hands. He caused rain when it was needed and warded off the rain clouds when they were likely to cause hindrance to people.

Bhagwan Ji also intervened in national and international affairs such as at the time of the Pak aggression in Kashmir in 1947, during the Sino-Indian conflict in 1962 and at the time of the Indo-Pak war of 1965. Some people also mention that more recently, he was seen in his physical form guiding the Indian soldiers to victory in the Kargil conflict of 2001.

In one of the many anecdotes reported, it is said that the wife of Shri Chuni Lal, Vice-Principal of a music college in Srinagar suffered from Leukaemia. She was under the treatment of an eminent cancer specialist. At one stage, based on her blood report, the doctor gave up all hope of her survival and discharged her thinking her end was near. Dejected and distressed, Chuni Lal went to Bhagawan Ji, who gave him a small packet of ashes from his *dhooni.* With tearful eyes, he said, 'What will these ashes do to my dying wife? Visibly moved Bhagawan Ji said that she should take the ashes with water or medicine. Chuni Lal went home skeptical about the efficacy of the ashes. He, however, told everything to his mother who snatched the tiny packet from his hand and put some ashes on the patient's tongue, smearing her body with the rest. The patient went off to sleep immediately. Waking up after two or three hours, she said that she was feeling hungry. Since it was late in the night, they could only feed her some milk. The next day her appetite had returned and she relished her food and felt much stronger. The doctor advised a fresh blood check-up. The check-up revealed a normal blood count with no trace of cancer. The doctor was puzzled and enquired of Chuni Lal what he had done and how she had been cured. Chuni Lal related the story about the ashes given by Bhagwan Ji. It appears, subsequently, the doctor also went to pay obeisance to Bhagawan Ji.

In another similar kind of story, a lady in Delhi was declared a case of pyelonephritis. The tests revealed that the infection in the kidney was galloping and destroying healthy tissues. A relative of the lady approached Bhagawan Ji in Srinagar with the prayer to save her, as her death would mean the ruin of her three young children. Bhagawan Ji was moved, filled his *chillum* and smoked it for about half-an-hour and said, "Go, the lady is saved". Her husband reported later that her further tests revealed that she was recovering. She recovered fully and led a normal life as a housewife.

Bhagwan Ji was kind and compassionate towards his devotees. He would empty his purse for the marriage of the daughter of a needy devotee and meet the requirements of the wedding. Though he would get furious to see an unchaste man or a woman of doubtful character, he would still show compassion towards all erring persons. Bhagwan Ji had no sense of ego. He always used the word 'we' instead of 'I'.

He taught that expansion of the ego to cosmic dimensions led to *Omkar,* the primordial sound and self-realisation. When he looked at the sky, he would see *devatas* in the form of bundles of conscious light.

Even today, when he has ceased to exist in human form, for all Kashmiri Pandits Bhagwan Ji is as radiant as the sun and as cool and soothing as the moon. He is deep as an ocean and vast as the sky. He is ever fresh as the morning dew. He provides shelter like a mighty banyan tree to all of us. Who knows our exile was also a way of keeping us safe and protected us till we could safely return? Whenever we see his portrait, picture or statue, a strange magnetic attraction is felt. We are drawn to him by the intense gaze of his eyes. We believe he is there to guide us from darkness to light.

Bhagwan Gopinath Ji Satsang Mandals have been established in Jammu, Allahabad, Delhi, Bangalore and other parts of India. In honour of Bhagwan Ji, the Government of India released a centenary postal stamp on 3rd July, 1998.

*"Bhagwan Ji Karin asisarinayBatanPyethPanunAnugreh thavinasisarinayrutczvath"*

□

# Swami Nand Bab—A Mystic Called Defense Minister of Kashmir

Kashmir has produced many saints and mystics with the power of clairvoyance who could not only read the present and the past, but also predict future events. One name amongst them would be Swami Nand Lal Ji who was one in the line of great seers produced by the valley of Kashmir over the centuries. He was popularly known by his homely name of 'Nand Bab'. 'Nand' is an abbreviation of his name Nand Lal and 'Bab' means father or an elder in the family. He was indeed a father figure to all.

His devotees had profound faith and unfathomable reverence for him. Every word he uttered was impregnated with deep meaning and was of great consequence for those who sought his blessings. If he chose, he would easily relieve the faithful who sought his protection from the mundane trials and tribulations that momentarily afflict every individual and disturb his or her equilibrium.

Swamiji was born on 30th December, 1896, at Purshayar, Habbakadal, Srinagar to Pandit Shanker Sahib and Shrimati Imberzal. Imberzal had a sister in Nunar, a village near Ganderbal. Since she had no issue of her own, she adopted Nand Lal. Even as a child, Nand Lal's face always radiated with spiritual grace.

He was educated by his adopted mother and was fairly

conversant in writing English, Urdu and Persian in a beautiful calligraphic style. After finishing his education, he joined the Police Department and was posted as a *Mohrarir*—a clerk in Pukhribal Police Station near the temple of Goddess. It is said that Swamiji had the vision of Goddess Sharika at this very place.

One day, one of his colleagues advised him to remain in the office properly dressed in his uniform as a Senior Police Officer was to visit the station the next day. The next day, ignoring this advice, Swamiji went to Devi-Angan, Goddess Sharika's temple and got absorbed in deep meditation. It was witnessed by some of his colleagues. However, when the Inspecting Officer visited the station, Swamiji was present at the station to the astonishment of all. They were amazed that he was present at both places simultaneously. From this date on, the miracles of the Swamiji started coming to light.

After some time, Swamiji was transferred to Tangadhar Police Station. He was not happy to go there and joined against his wishes. One day, without taking permission, Swamiji left Tanghadar on foot for Srinagar. On the way, he met a British officer who was wearing a hat. Swamiji removed his hat and put it on his head. Legal action was instituted against him for insulting a British Officer. He was dismissed from the State Police Service. From that day, he wore a hat for the rest of his life.

Wherever Nand Bab lived, he was mobbed by people of all faiths who sought his blessings, right from dawn to midnight. Even people coming from foreign countries would go to him. He would seldom talk directly to anyone present in the audience. He would answer an unspoken-query in the mind of one person by directing the reply to another person. He would talk in parables, similes, paradoxes and metaphors but not directly. At times, he laughed or sang, but generally, he would be dictating something or the other to anyone present on chits of paper or in a register kept for this purpose.

The writings on these chits or in the register would usually be replies to the queries and problems in the minds of the people present among the audience. These could also contain solutions to other matters of public importance. All these answers were given in metaphorical language.

Nand Bab had passed that highest stage or *siddhi* of spiritual evolution and had acquired the power of clairvoyance. He could enumerate problems and make prophecies of personal, social as well as of political nature with precision. Suffice to say that he could read the mind of people around him and understand what bothered them and often offered solutions too. He would take particular care of those whom he considered to be his main devotees or in his own words, who were under his banner, his *Alam.*

As per the Ashram sources, many miracles are attributed to Nand Bab. A young man, Mr. Qasba in U.S.A. got his pancreas damaged in a car accident. At one stage, the hospital declared his condition very serious. His family in Srinagar were informed telephonically about the accident and his deteriorating condition. His uncle got restless and could not sleep a wink during the night. Early next morning, he went to Swamiji, who was staying across the street.

Sensing the agony of Qasba's uncle, Swamiji said, "How will one live on an empty stomach" implying that the victim was not given any food to eat. After a few days at another place nearby, Swamiji said, "Bring some tea for us to drink." Qasba's uncle asked the victim's mother to comply. A third time, *Kheer*—a rice pudding was demanded by Swamiji. This too was complied with. This was followed by the request for solid food which was also arranged. Dates of all these events had been recorded by the people concerned. Direct telephone calls were exchanged between Srinagar and the U.S.A. On his return for a short sojourn to the Valley after his full recovery, Mr. Qasba, the accident victim confirmed the dates of his steady recovery and when he was administered glucose, given tea to drink and given semi-solid and solid food to eat.

Nand Bab had a double personality. With his nearest disciples, his behaviour usually was that of a normal human being; he would talk about their personal matters, advise them on their family affairs and listen to them with patience and affection. At other times, he would be in his super-conscious state. He would not give any straight replies to any questions or requests.

Nand Bab's movements would be unpredictable. He would leave his residence usually in a car, taxi or in a *tonga* and direct the driver to take him from place to place. At times, such trips would continue for days and cover various cities and destinations. Once in Jammu, he took a taxi for Delhi. On the way, the petrol tank of the taxi became dry and it stopped. Nand Bab asked the driver why he had stopped the vehicle. The driver informed him that the taxi had run out of petrol.

Swamiji asked if he had any water, he should pour it into the petrol tank. The poor driver, more out of awe for the Swamiji, poured water into the petrol tank. The taxi started straight away. It reached Delhi without any petrol in its tank. This incident was narrated to Shri J.N. Bhat by the taxi driver himself and is reported by him in his article published in Koshur Samachar.

Nand Bab could predict the rise and fall of various governments. Some mystics even addressed him as 'the Defence Minister of Kashmir.' It was also believed that a host of other mystics, unknown and unidentifiable, worked under him at different levels and different posts to assist him. Later on, his mystical jurisdiction extended to entire India.

Shri J.N. Bhat mentions some true incidents, looking apparently unbelievable. In 1965, when Pakistan invaded

Kashmir, Nand Bab was staying in the house of Pandit Balkak Dhar, his disciple. He started burning a huge fire and kept awake the whole night, sometimes weeping, sometimes laughing and sometimes crying.

In the morning when Shri J.N. Bhat met him, Nand Bab said that the previous night was the most difficult one for me, "They wanted to invade the airport and I had to fight hard for changing their route." What had transpired was an actual attack by the Pakistani raiders who had made all attempts during the previous night to capture the airfield but had failed. While Pakistan Saber Jet flew over Srinagar, Swamiji kept performing a *havan*. When people were panicking, he reprimanded them and assured them that nothing would happen. When he was pressed further by queries, he got a little irritated and said, "I have told you nothing will happen; should I give you in writing on a stamp paper?"

He made miraculously amazing predictions during the wars of 1947, 1962, 1965, 1971. For example, during the Chinese War one day, he said "Shahi Cheena, Fish Kar Lutak" and the next day, there was a ceasefire.

Sati-Ded, popularly known as Sati *Macha,* was a contemporary of Swamiji. She lived at Tankypora, Habbakadal. It was this lady-saint who had predicted the present exodus of the Kashmiri Pandits with the words: "*Batni Watnuk Loal Mai Oai*". Swamiji also had predicted exodus when he had gone to Acha Bal to meet his disciples there.

In his madness, there was a method; in his ramblings were deep philosophy; in his wanderings, the discharge of his political responsibilities; in his reveries and prayers, the solicitude of his needy, the diseased devotees. He was celestial, he was benevolent, he was magnanimous and above all, he was universal.

He happens to be the guru of my father and I listen to many similar experiences from my dad as well. His *simran* or his remembrance or a blissful thought about him gives me confidence. I feel we Kashmiri Pandits are surely protected by his blessings and we should continue to have faith in his spiritual power and strength. He continues to be with us even now. Swamiji left his mortal coil on 10th October, 1973 at Delhi after a brief illness. Swami Nand Bab Asharam has been established at Laley-De-Bagh.

*Excerpts taken from Shri J.N. Bhat's article and Stories published by Swamiji's Ashram in Jammu.*

□

# Swami Kashkak—Head of the Spiritual Government of Kashmir

*Kashyapver* has always been known for its Shakti cult. Many sages and seers have attained enlightenment through their devotion, creative spirits and sheer practice. In the last millennium, Kashmir has produced a galaxy of mystics, saints, seers and savants who have enriched, elevated and refined life and helped the people in distress at large. We Kashmiri Pandits are fortunate to belong to the land of Lalleshwari, Rupa Bhawani, Parmanand, Rishipir, Jeewan Shah, Lassa Sahib, Swami Anandji, Swami Ramji, Sahib Kaul, Manas Razdan, Zaikak, Kakaji Mastana, Grata Bab, Ramjoo Tabardar, Vidya Dar, Shankar Razdan, Bhagawaan Gopinathji, Sona Kak, Swami Nand Lal Ji, Swami Lakshmanjoo, Sati Devi, Mathura Devi and Swami Kashkak and many more and it is through their continued blessings that we have stood up and fought back every time whenever we have fallen.

These saints transcended the bonds of our community and provided their blessings and guidance from time to time. In the present troubled times when Kashmiri Pandits, in particular, are passing through untold miseries, the only solace comes from our glorious philosophic and spiritual traditions enriched by our saints. One of these personalities was Swami Kashkak in whose presence people found comfort and solace.

In mystic tradition, it is believed that a sort of divine

government functions on earth at different points in time. This kind of set-up is said to be manned by known and unknown seers and sages from time to time. Swami Kashkak was said to have been the head of such a spiritual set-up in Kashmir during his lifetime. After him, the mantle was passed on to Bhagawaan Gopinathji.

Swamiji was born in 1880 in the village of Mani Gaon. Before him, it was Mata Rupa Bhawani who had hallowed the tiny village during the days of her early penance in the late 17th century. Swamiji was initiated into the yogic discipline by his guru, Narayan Bhan, a Siddha yogi of his time. This enabled him to attain *siddhis*-self-realisation, at a very young age. Once in a trance, Swamiji climbed a tree wearing his wooden clogs.

Kashkak cared very little for his body. He refused any sort of treatment if he was unwell. He had developed a permanent deep sore on one of his legs but he never accepted any treatment for it. Dr. Sidhnath Kaul, a well-known doctor from Delhi came all the way to persuade and plead with him to take treatment but Kashkak rejected the plea with the usual cryptic remark: "Well it is not a sore as you think; it is a gift that God has given me. Better leave it like that."

In one of the incidents, it is said that once a *Gujjar,* who had sustained a fracture in his right arm came to Kashkak and implored, "Bab (father), take pity on me please; be kind and heal my arm. This is the harvesting season and down and out as I am, my family will die of starvation if I am not alright." The compassionate sage touched the fractured arm and, lo and behold, it was restored to the normal. The *Gujjar* sped away in joy.

Another farmer seated there protested saying that the *Gujjar* did not deserve Bab's kindness, as he was known for his cunningness. Pat came the saint's reply: "You won't understand all this. We are here to help and serve those in trouble; we are here to simplify and not complicate matters. If the *Gujjar*'s arm was not cured immediately, his family, his innocent children, would have suffered for no fault of

theirs. If indeed, as you say, the *Gujjar* is a bad person, he cannot escape the fruit of his moral lapses. He will have to go through hell after the harvest season is over." This actually happened. It was learnt later that *Gujjar's* trouble returned after harvest season was over and he had to go through the painful medical procedure.

In another incident, it is mentioned that the parents of an unfortunate youth brought him to Manigam. They had travelled by *tonga* from Srinagar. The youth had stopped urinating and had a distended bladder. The doctors had given up on him in despair. The parents tearfully entreated Kashkak to intervene but Bab refused, saying that his ailment was the result of his past karma. The parents would not take no for an answer and went on pleading. Finally, Kashkak relented and said that they could go back and someone else would bear the youth's karma.

Hardly had their *tonga* gone a few kilometres, when the young man stopped it, descended to the roadside and passed several litres of urine and was cured of his ailment. However, immediately thereafter, the horse fell dead.

Kashkak exercised his healing touch whenever and wherever necessary. He wielded his spiritual powers, the *ashta siddhis* to serve humanity and provide succour and solace to the afflicted souls. It was said of him that he fulfilled everyone's wishes and never disappointed anyone.

A mere glance of this saint brought comfort and solace to everyone. As his fame spread far and wide, crowds from all walks of life thronged the village day in and day out to pay their respects and to seek his divine favours. Those visiting him included not only, the common men, women and children, but also rich businessmen, top government officials and even Maharaja Hari Singh, the ruler of Kashmir. Even saints and mystics had great faith in him and revered him.

In the first week of August 1953, Swami Nand Lal Ji, attired in usual military uniform with a toy gun in hand, stationed himself in the state secretariat just outside the office of Sheikh Mohammed Abdullah, the then *Prime Minister* of Kashmir. The visitors to the secretariat bore witness to the fact that the bizarre mystic had his gun pointed toward Sheikh Abdullah's office all the while.

Meanwhile, he sent one of his devotees to Kashkak with an envelope, as if to seek his approval for something about which no one could make even the slightest guess at that time. It was, perhaps, one of the many 'mysterious' consultations Nand Bab would often hold with Kashkak on matters of grave importance of the state and the country as a whole.

What happened on 9 August, 1953, is now a matter of history. Sheikh Abdullah was unceremoniously deposed on that day.

Kashkak's predictions were often shrouded in ambiguity. To a query as to when a particular gentleman would get married, he replied, '*Yora gachhith ta tora yith*', meaning after he died and was reborn. That gentleman remained a bachelor all his life.

Kashkak was a married man, a *grihastha.* He led a very simple, normal life of an ordinary householder, earning his daily bread by toiling in the fields and by tilling whatever little land he possessed till the end of his life.

Despite being a poor farmer, he always refused offerings, whether in kind or cash. He threw whatever was offered to him into the Sindhu River, which flowed nearby. Yet he displayed utmost hospitality. Those coming from far spent night at his place and were served a simple meal of rice, curd, dal and vegetables. He treated the rich and poor alike and never discriminated. Kashkak attained *mahasamadhi* on 17th August, 1961.

Let's rekindle the flame of our spiritual masters of Kashmir whose blessings is going to provide us strength and help our community to be successful collectively.

*Excerpts from the write-ups of Dr. S. Radhakrishnan, Shri G.N. Raina, Koshur Samachar, Picture from Anjali Kaul, Austin.*

□

# Part-5

# Festivals

# Mitra Poornima—The Festival of Friendship

Before the advent of Islam, Kashmiri Pandits celebrated a unique festival of friendship. It fell on the day of Mitra Poornima, the full moon of the month of Ashvin. On that night, a lamp was burnt, in the honour of Mitra, a Vedic God. Mitra is the patron deity of honesty, friendship, contracts and meetings. He is the protector of treaties and promises and the guardian of friendships. He is the principal guardian of truth and order and he abhors all violence. Mitra also refers to the morning sun. The Sanskrit word 'Mitra for friend' is derived from this Vedic God.

The following morning was known as Mitra Prabhat, the morning of Mitra. On this day, fresh lotuses, rose petals and marigolds, washed in the water of the Vitasta were offered to Mitra along with walnuts, fruits, and milk products. These were kept on a decorated platter in his honour.

The children were also given a bath in the Vitasta and dressed in bright red, yellow or orange silk robes to represent the radiance and the glory of Mitra. Games were organised for children so that they are encouraged to forge friendships and develop team spirit. To show friendship and fellowship to all, the clothes and quilts were donated to the needy and poor. The *prasad* of sweets and fruits offered to Mitra was also shared with them. The lotus stems of fresh lotuses emerging from the pristine water bodies were cooked and eaten on that day as a special dish.

This festival of ancient Kashmir is a unique festival that glorifies the meaning and essence of friendship. It indicates the type of culture we have, which emphasises forging trustworthiness, non-violence, sharing and goodwill. The festival stopped after violent and unfriendly forces gripped Kashmir. We strongly feel we need to revive the Mitra festival not only among Kashmiris but across the globe. Nowadays, people in the West have started celebrating Friendship Day, while Kashmiri Pandits had a tradition of celebrating friendship from the Vedic times.

□

# Kechi Mavas Yaksha Amavasya

Kashmiris follow numerous rituals, traditions and festivals of proto-Vedic origin. The communities living in Kashmir, from the time of the Neolithic age of Burzahom, comprised Nagas, Yakshas and Pisachas who formed the local cultural denominations. Rituals like *Gada-Batta, Kaw Punim, Khechi Mavas, Herath* and more have an ancient past and are symbolic of a theological philosophy. Many of them have been prescribed by Nil Nag, the King of Nagas in Nilamat Purana to be followed by the new settlers to honour local people and local traditions.

During our childhood days in Kashmir, on one of the festive *Amavasya* nights, the lentils cooked with rice-*khichdi* was kept outside the door for the *yech* to feast on. *Yech* is an expression used for Yakhshas and Pishachas—the ancient indigenous people of Kashmir who were given a demi-god status. We were told that a *yech* wearing a golden cap would visit our house to eat the *khichdi* and whosoever managed to steal the golden cap of the *yech* would get all the riches of the world. While some of us would be fascinated with the idea and would do all the planning to snatch the cap, the others would be terrified and would want to keep away from the *yech*. We would stay awake late into the night, peeping through the windows, eyes glued on the large plate full of *khichdi*. However, none ever saw the *yech* as most of the children fell asleep while waiting.

This ancient ritual of the Kashmiri Pandits known as

*Kechi Mavas* or *khichdi* Amavasya dates back to times immemorial and is celebrated on the no-moon day–*Amavasya* of the Hindu month of *Pausha*. On this day, *Khichdi* is offered to Kubera as sacrificial food. Kubera is the God of wealth and the Lord of semi-divine yakshas. He is supposed to be the regent of the north *Dig-Pala* and protector of the world *Lok-Pala*. In the night, a pestle or any other stone is washed and anointed with sandalwood paste and vermilion. As a symbol of Lord Kubera, he is worshipped with the chanting of mantras and the *Khichdi* is offered to him along with radish and pickle as *naivedya*. After the Pooja is over, a portion of *naivedya* is kept on the outer wall of his house by the worshipper in the belief that *Yaksha* will come to eat it. The rest of the food is eaten by the family members as *Prasad*.

This ritual is the yearly re-enactment of the peace treaty that was made between the demi-god and the humans in Kashmir after Rishi Kashyap settled 'sons of Manu', the Brahmins in Kashmir to live alongside the Nagas, Yakshas and Pisachas, the indigenous communities of Kashmir. New settlers to show gratitude for the forest tribes and communities that already existed in Kashmir made thanksgiving offerings. It is also said that in winter, forest tribes experienced a shortage of food. Hence, there were several festivals in winter where food was offered to them and *Khech Mavas* is one of them.

On this day of Paush, when the yakshas descended from the mountains, the new settlers did not wish to neglect their needs and made arrangements to satisfy their hunger. The food was served to them as per the ancient agreement so that yakshas would not bother humans during tough winters and everyone will reside in the valley in peace and harmony. Thus the festival commemorates the coming together and co-mingling of various races and ethnic groups in prehistoric Kashmir. The offering of *khichdi* has continued for several thousand years as a part of our rich cultural heritage.

In contrast to the west, where new settlers in North and South America, Canada and Australia tried to exterminate the aboriginal communities and treated them most harshly, the Kashmiri culture in contrast comes as a whiff of fresh air and needs to be emulated worldwide.

Over the millenniums, *Manavs*, Nagas, Yakshas and Pisachas seem to have become harmonised and mainstreamed. They no more descend from the mountains during harsh winter. However, the agreement is still symbolically honoured by the Kashmiri Pandits indicating thanksgiving, gratitude, hospitality and harmony.

Interestingly, the festival called *Khichdi* is celebrated throughout India in the same season as a harvest festival. A simple fare of the rice with lentils, *khichdi* or *Pongal* is made with the newly harvested rice, offered to folk and village Gods and eaten as *prasad.* In South India, it is a major four-day harvest festival and is celebrated as Pongal. In Assam, it is Bihu, in Punjab, it is Lohri, in UP and Maharashtra and other places, it is celebrated as Makar Sankranti or *Khichdi.* It also marks the first day of the sun's transit into the Vedic Zodiac of Makar Rashi (Capricorn), marking the end of the month with the winter solstice and the start of longer days.

*Is our Yaksha waiting for Khichdi?*

*Excerpts from Nilamata Purana, Dr. Ved Kumari Ghai and other available writings.*

□

# Hyerath-Shivratri

## Herath-Hari Ratri or Shivaratri

Shivaratri is known as Herath, or Hari Ratri—the night of Hari, another name for Shiva. Herath is celebrated to commemorate Lord Shiva's marriage to Parvati or the union of Shiva and Shakti. It is symbolic of the union of Atma (individual soul) with Paramatma (the Supreme) and represents the higher state of spiritual realisation wherein the seeker becomes fully aware of his oneness with Shiva and experiences Eternal Truth, Bliss and Beauty, known as *Satyam, Shivam, Sundaram*. The 9th century Kashmiri saint-poet, Utpal Deva, describes Shivaratri thus:

> "When the sun, the moon and all the other stars set at the same time, there arises the radiant night of Shiva, spreading a splendour of its own. On this day, in India, devotees pray, sing, observe a fast and offer coconuts, Bilva leaves, fruits, and sacred food to Shiva and his divine consort Parvati."

Many stories are connected with the origin of Shivaratri. One of them is about the churning of the divine Ksheer Sagar-the Ocean of Milk. When the *devas* (gods) and *asuras* (demons) were churning the ocean to obtain amrita (nectar of immortality), they came across the deadly poison, *Kalakuta.* As soon as they touched it, it exploded into poisonous fumes that threatened to destroy the universe. The gods ran for assistance to Brahma and Vishnu who were unable to help. At last, they begged Shiva to save them. Shiva raised his trident and condensed the poisonous fumes. He swallowed the poison without spilling a single drop, to save the universe. His consort, Parvati put her hand on Shiva's throat to stop the poison from percolating into his body. The poison remained in Shiva's throat. His throat became blue and he came to be known as Neelkantha, the blue-throated one. The gods worship Shiva for saving Creation, on this auspicious day.

## Story about Vatuk Pooja

In Kashmir, Shivaratri means undertaking an elaborate Vatuka Pooja, which lasts for days. The tantric texts describe Shivaratri as Bhairavotsava and explain the worship of Vatuk. The main aspect is the worship of Shiva and Parvati as *Bhairava* and *Bhairavi* and their sons Ganesh and Kumar, as Vatuk *Bhairava* and Rama Bhairava and propitiating them through the *tantric* rites. One legend about the origin of Vatuk Pooja is that on this day, a *Jwala Linga* appeared at Pradoshakala (at dusk) as a blazing column of fire and dazzled young Vatuk Bhairava and Rama Bhairava (Ganesh and Kumar), the manasputras (sons born of their mental resolve) of Parvati. They approached *Jawala Linga* to discover its beginning and its end but could not fathom it. Exasperated, they went to inform their mother Parvati about the presence of Jwala Linga. Parvati, herself merged with the awe-inspiring Jwala-linga but before that she blessed both Vatuk Bhairava and Rama Bhairava that they would be worshipped by human beings and would receive their share of sacrificial offerings on this day. Those who worship them would have all their wishes fulfilled.

According to another theory, when Kashmiri Pandits were driven out of the valley in the first half of the 15th century, a few families stayed back in remote rural areas. It is believed that they started the tradition of worship of Vatuka Bhairava (Ganesh) to invoke his protection.

## Vatuk Pantheon

The Vatuk pantheon comprises of an array of earthen pots. The two big earthen pitchers, filled with walnuts soaked in water and flowers, represent Shiva and Parvati. Two smaller pots denote Vatuk Bhairava and Rama Bhairava. Apart from these, a definite number of small earthen pots containing walnuts and water symbolize Shiva's Ganas, Nandi, Yoginis, Kshetrapalas, Vagur and Sonipotul, and other deities. These pots, collectively, are called Vatuk. They are symbolic of Shiva and his entourage and are worshipped every day during the festival and food offered to them.

As part of Shivaratri celebrations, elaborate tantric rituals are performed during the day and fire pooja is performed during the night. The festival is observed for 23 days, starting from the first day of the dark fortnight of the Hindu month of *Phalgun*, called Hurya Akodoh in Kashmir, and ends on the eighth day of the bright fortnight of Phalgun, known as *Teel Aatham* (til Ashtami). The Vedic hymns and mantras about Shiva are chanted individually and collectively throughout this period. Before migration, the Kashmiri Pandits homes used to vibrate with the chant of:

*Namah Sambhavaya Cha,*
*Mayo Bhavaya Cha,*
*Namah Sankaraya Cha,*
*Mayas Karaya Cha,*
*Namah Sivaya Cha,*
*Sivtaraya Cha.*

### Hurey Akodah to Hurey Shaiyam

The first six days are dedicated to cleaning the entire house to give it a festive look as well as collecting pooja items like mud pots, walnuts and other pooja paraphernalia.

### Hurey Satam, Aatham and Navam

During the seventh, eighth and ninth day, devotional prayers and chanting were continued.

### Dyare Daham

On the tenth day called Dyare Daham, the married women and newlywed daughters and daughters-in-law are sent to their homes, laden with the auspicious cheer and gifts for the family and in-laws. It is believed that every girl symbolizes Parvati, wedded to Shiva, and is shown due respect on this festive occasion.

### Gaadkah

The 11th day of the festival is called the festival of fish. It is dedicated to the worship of Bhairavas by offering fish. Barring a few, in most families, fish is cooked and eaten after offering to the Bhairavas first. Some families make a vegetarian offering instead.

## Vagarye Bah and Vatuk Barun

On the 12th day, the earthen pots are ceremoniously brought home and placed on a special pedestal in a sanctified place. The pots are then filled with water, walnuts and flowers. This ceremony is known as *Vatuk Barun,* meaning filling the pots.

## Herath Truvah

The main Shivaratri Pooja is done on the 13th day of the dark fortnight of the month of Phalgun. Night long prayers are held and many observe a fast. Our parents and grandparents always fasted on this day and meditated through the night, after fire-worship. Traditionally, everyone kept awake on that night including children. Thus, while elders were engaged in prayers, the youngsters would play with Kori shells through the night to keep awake.

Our parents have fond memories of playing with Kori shells on the nights leading to Shivaratri. The choicest dishes, mainly of meat and fish, are cooked as sacrificial food and eaten after offering to the Vatuk pantheon. The food is symbolically offered to all the Vatuk pots. Offering and eating meat and fish on Shivaratri is strictly a Kashmiri Pandit ritual, to propitiate the 'Bhairavas'. According to the Shiva Samhita, it is auspicious to consume sacrificial food and to break the fast after the pooja.

## Donya Mayas—Distribution of Prasad

On the next day, the 14th day, called 'Walnut New Moon' the walnuts from the pitchers are distributed to relatives and friends. After immersion of pots in the river, the soaked walnuts are brought back after a symbolic pooja on the bank of the river. The walnuts are broken to take the kernel out and along with *Tomul Chhot*, the *rotis* made of rice flour, they are first offered to the deity and then distributed as *prasad* among family, friends, and neighbours. The closer the relationship, the larger is the number of walnuts given to them. The highest number, in hundreds, goes to the in-laws of the newly-wed daughters. The use of soaked walnut as *prasad* is unique to Kashmir. Walnut becomes new by soaking and tastes fresh, symbolizing regeneration of something considered dead.

## Herath Kharch

Herath Kharch (gift of money) is a custom of giving money by the elders to all members of the family, on the following morning, to have fun. Just like Eidi is given on the occasion of Eid, youngsters look forward to receiving the Herath Kharch. On the social side, there is great joy all around. People wear new clothes and families sit together to enjoy the game of Kori shells.

## Dub-Dub–Knock-Knock

A very interesting ritual, called Dub-Dub or Knock-Knock is enacted in the evening. One member of the family goes out and returns with a glass of water. When he knocks on the door, he is asked, "Who is it?" He would reply, "Ram Bror (Rama's cat)." They ask, "What have you brought?" He replies, "I have come with wealth, health, happiness, food and means of livelihood and all the good things." After hearing this, the door is opened and he is allowed into the house as a messenger of prosperity and good luck. This marks the grand finale of this great festival.

## Salaam

On the next day of Shivaratri, the Muslim friends would come to greet the Pandits, wishing them a happy year ahead and greet them with a Salaam. Probably, that is the reason it has been celebrated as Salaam Day, also the day for paying social visits to friends and relatives to greet them and wish them. In past, the relatives and friends were invited for a sumptuous meal on the day of Salaam.

In our childhood in old Srinagar, we have seen Muslim bards, street dancers, Kuil faquirs and dancing dervishes visiting the households of Pandits to greet and entertain them with their music and dance. They also claimed their due share of the festival in cash or kind and saluted our elders with the words 'Salaam'. 'Salaam' was the Muslim way of celebrating Shivaratri along with their Hindu neighbours.

## Tila Aatham (Til Ashtami)

The festival ends on the Phalgun Krishna Ashtami called Tila Aatham. On the evening of this day, people wind up the pooja paraphernalia and take it to the River Vitasta, for immersion. In the evening, a game of burning old used fire pots *kangris* called Jat-tun-tun is played. The old Kangris are burnt and thrown into the river while children shout Jat-tun-tun meaning there is a flame. This signifies the end of the winter.

Many Kashmiri families for centuries have been

observing elaborate Vatuk Pooja every Shivaratri, despite living outside Kashmir for decades or more. In days gone by, even walnuts had to be parcelled from Kashmir for pooja. Today, when we have dispersed around the globe, we have to find ways and means to keep our traditions alive.

□

# Navreh Kashmiri New Year

'Navreh', the Kashmiri Pandits' New Year, reflects the age-old social, ethnic, cultural and religious ethos that usher us into the freshness of the New Year. It falls on the first day of the *Sapatrishi Samvat* of the lunar year, in the Indian month of *Chaitra*. The 'Brahma Purana' says that the universe was created by Lord Brahma on this day. As per the *Matsya Purana*, this is the day when Lord Vishnu, was incarnated in the form of a giant fish 'Matsya Avtar'. The festival of `Navreh' signifies the beginning of *Satya Yuga*, the golden era in Hindu mythology. It also signals the starting of *Vikram Samvats* to commemorate the victory of Chandra Gupta Maurya over the `Shalkas'. Al Beruni, a medieval traveller, has mentioned in his work, *Kitabul Hind,* that the month of Chaitra denotes festivities for the natives of Kashmir, on account of the victory gained by an ancient Kashmiri King Lalitaditya over the Turks.

It is also hailed as the beginning of spring' Basant' or 'Sonth' in Kashmir. Noted cultural scholar, Shri Opinder Ambardar, describes the coming of the spring thus:

"With the coming of *Sonth* in Kashmir, the fresh life spurts in the fields to forests, new foliage blossoms, and a riot of colours in the form of flowers make their presence everywhere. Beautiful and sweet-scented *Eamberzal* or Narcissus flower makes its appearance as soon as the snow melts in the valley and announces the arrival of spring in Kashmir.

The early migratory birds such as *'Phemb-Seer'* (Paradise Flycatcher), *'Poshnool'* *(*Golden Oriole*), Kukil* (Ring-Dove), *'Katij'* (common swallow), *'TsiniHangur'* (Himalayan Sterling) and *'Sheen-pipin'* (Pied-Wagtail) also proclaim the advent of *Sonth'* in Kashmir through their melodious notes.

Navreh is a celebration of the change of season, regeneration and fertility, a journey from cold to warmth, an escape from winter confinement to social communion, and a beginning of new lease of life. It is the time to bid adieu to harsh winter and welcome the warmth of spring to thank the overwhelming generosity of nature, which is visible everywhere. The display of new life in nature and invigorating ambience arouses hope and inspiration, even in the most brazen hearts".

In the words of celebrated historian Srivara, the Chaitra festival in ancient Kashmir was laced with enthusiasm and fervour to the accompaniment of lighting of lamps and merriment everywhere.

The day before the Navreh, Kashmiri Pandits visited Vicharnag Shrine, about eight kilometres from Srinagar, to offer prayers, after having a holy dip in the spring. Traditionally, on this day, the annual Almanac, *Panchang* was released for the public after being approved by the learned Pandits at Vicharnag. The newly released almanac was brought to our homes by Kul-Guru along with *'Kreel Pach'*, an illustrated scroll having a picture of the family deity, which is either Goddess Saraswati or Goddess Sharika, with a hymn in her praise written underneath.

On the eve of Navreh, the lady of the house would fill a *Thaal* with raw and cooked rice, walnuts and almonds, paddy, a piece of bread, a pen and inkpot, a book, a cup of curd, money/silver coin, gold ornament, a pinch of salt, seasonal flowers, such as *Yamberzal,* a herb called `*Vai*' or `Sweet flag', a mirror and a photograph of the family deity. She arranges these along with the *'Nachhipatar'* and the *Kreel-Pach'*. This ritual is known as *'Thaal-Bharun,* filling the *Thaal* with the tokens of auspiciousness. On the morning of `Navreh', the daughter of the house, would make everyone in the family have a *darshan'* of the *Thaal* as the first act of the day, by taking it around the house. Alternatively, the *Thaal* can be placed at a convenient place in the living area, and everybody is reminded to have *darshan* of the *thaal,* immediately after waking up in the morning, as the first thing. This is known as *Buth-Vuchun.* This ritual is said to bring health, wealth, wisdom and good luck for the entire family. Every elder member of the family puts some money in the *Thaal* which is then taken by the girl, as a gift known as *'Kharch'* or pocket money.

Shri Opinder Ambardar vividly describes the significance of various objects in the *Thaal,* thus:

There is a belief that a mysterious power lies hidden in all human beings. It can be stimulated by the use of specific symbols as our subconscious correlates better with the symbols in comparison to the words. All these items have symbolic significance. Rice, the principal diet of Kashmiris, is a symbol of abundance, life, growth, development, expansion and prosperity. It is an integral part of every auspicious occasion in our lives. It also stands for refinement and purity in individual life. Paddy connotes unsullied clarity, natural perfection and untainted life, without deception and imitation. Cooked rice indicates a metaphoric process through which paddy has passed up to the cooked form. As such, the cooked rice is a symbol of transformation and progression in life in the right direction. Besides, the cooked rice is regarded as a *prasad* and gift of God to mankind. The paddy, rice and cooked rice are the sources of survival and sustenance of our physical and mental growth.

Curd is a symbolic representation of fullness, stability and cohesiveness in life. Due to its '*Satvic*' quality, curd also represents placidity, consistency and virtuous conduct in life. The bread is a symbolic representation for absorption, expansion and integration in one's socio-cultural surroundings. The walnuts and almonds indicate regeneration, evolutionary process, continuity and flow of life. The four kernels present in the walnut represent the four aspects of *dharma* or divinity, namely wealth or *arth, kama* or wish fulfilment and *moksha* or salvation. Money represents good fortune, prosperity, wealth and material strength. The gold is a symbol of purity and auspiciousness. It has religious and spiritual significance as it not only gives contentment but drives away evil influences. The money and gold ornament together remind us not to shun righteousness in the pursuit of material wealth. The medicinal herb of '*Vai*' is symbolic of leading a disease-free life. *Flowers* represent freshness, hope, fragrance, compassion and feeling of concern in life. They are so inextricably associated with human life that no celebration or rejoicing is complete without them. They are also a symbol of the impermanence of life. Flowers rejuvenate the mood and drive one away from feelings of depression and dejection.

The pen, inkpot and the book taken together symbolise wisdom, knowledge, awareness, insight, and enlightenment, learning and intellectual brilliance. They also represent the power of knowledge for the eradication of illiteracy, ignorance and shallowness. They have the allegoric meaning for '*Apara Vidya*' i.e. knowledge of worldly objects and '*Para Vidya*' i.e. knowledge of the self. Salt, which is central to our day-to-day life, is supposed to generate positive energy and drive away bad luck. The sugar candy signifies cordial social bonding and sweetness at every stage in life.

The Jantri–New Year Calendar represents the symbolic connection of the events in human life to the planetary influences and their movements. '*Kreel Pach*' having a picture of *Isht Devi*, is indicative of religious bent, our trust in her grace and our total surrender to her sovereignty. Mirror, due to its attribute of reflection, stands for duplication of auspiciousness, as well as all the good events of life. The mirror is also believed to dispel and deflect the damaging impact and influences.

The Goddess Lakshmi is symbolically represented in her different aspects, as Vidyalakshmi represented by pen, inkpot and book, Dhanyalakshmi represented by paddy, rice, cooked rice, bread and curd and Dhanalakshmi represented by a coin, currency note and gold ornament. The various agriculture and cattle products represent Mother Nature, Mother Earth, `Bhoodevi' and Goddess Shakambhari, the Goddess of vegetation and agriculture. Besides it, Goddess Mahakali, the presiding deity of longevity, is represented by the medicinal herb of '*Vai.*

On the day of Navreh, the rice in the *Thaal* is used for making yellow coloured rice called *Taher*' which is eaten as *prasad or naveed,* after performing puja by the family members. On `Navreh' morning, the walnuts in the *Thaal* are dropped into the River as the flowing water of the river and walnuts together symbolically represents regeneration and continuity of a fruitful and productive life. It is also a metaphor for the surge and movement of active and energetic life".

In the good old days before the exodus in the 1990s, on `Navreh' morning, Kashmiri Pandits, after bathing and dressing in new clothes, would head towards Hari Parvat to pray to the Goddess Sharika, the presiding deity of Srinagar City. After visiting Hari Parvat, they would have a picnic at *Badam Vari,* the orchard of almonds, situated at its foothills. Here they would enjoy sipping steaming Kehwa made in Samavaar. They would also relish such delicacies as roasted water chestnuts, oil-fried Luchies and the lotus root *pakoras.* The children with beaming faces enjoyed playing with water-balls, gas-filled balloons and *Tikawavij*. On this day, the *Badam-Vari* looked like a fairyland due to the *Badam Phulai*, the almond blossom with trees full of pink and white flowers reminding one of the cherry blossoms in Japan. Almond is the first fruit-bearing tree to blossom in Kashmir to usher in spring.

Navreh has its special cuisines. The violet or green coloured leafy spring vegetable, locally called Vosta-Hak, cooked with radish or lotus stem, is a special dish of the Navreh feast. The cottage cheese cooked in combination with a native wild vegetable called '*Tsokalader*' is another prized dish of the day. Near and dear ones, especially daughters and sons-in-law are invited for the Navreh feast.

□

# Punn Dyun
# Celebrating Prosperity

The word punn in Kashmiri language means thread. According to a renowned Kashmiri scholar, 'Punn' festival was originally associated with the spinning of newly produced cotton and worshipping the twin agrarian local goddesses, Vibha and Garbha to whom *Roth,* sweet pancakes were offered.

The twin goddesses later seem to have merged into one another assuming the identity of the folk deity Beib Garabh Maej who is symbolically represented by a brass pitcher filled with water. A new cotton thread is tied to the neck of the pot and a handful of grass *(dramun)* is kept inside it. These two rituals indicate the ancient connection of the festival both with agriculture as well as with the newly spun cotton. Incidentally, spinning cotton and wool was a proud activity for Kashmiri women and every household possessed several spinning wheels (*charkhas*) since ancient times.

The punn festival is observed during the bright fortnight of Bhadra coinciding with *Ganesh Chaturthi*. Lord Ganesha occupies a special place amongst the Kashmiri Pandit worship and rituals. He has been blessed by Lord Shiva as 'Siddhi Daata' the giver of boons. Thus the Ganesh Pooja is an essential part of the festival. The brass pot filled with water representing the twin goddesses is placed in a clean spot early in the morning. For propitiating Lord Ganesha, the ladies of the house prepare sweet pancakes, *roths,* garnished with poppy seeds and ladoos made of wheat flour and ghee.

These are distributed after Pooja amongst relatives, neighbours and friends, which help our community to strengthen the social bonds. In the Kashmiri language, Vinayak Chaturthi is called 'Vinayak Choram'. It is considered most auspicious when the festival falls on a Sunday, which is celebrated as '*Vinayak Choram Te Aathwaar*'.

## Punn *Pooja*

The *roths* are kept in a basket covered with a cotton cloth. No one is allowed to touch or eat them before the *Pooja*. The pot of water symbolic of Goddesses is decorated with flower garlands, silver foil, *Narivan* and vermillion. The women children and family members gather around the pot. The lady of the house after giving the flowers, *akshat* grains and little fresh grass to hold, ties the protective *Narivan,* thread, around their wrists. One of the elders of the family narrates the story of 'Beeb Gharab Maej'. Once the narration of the story ends, the grass, flowers, rice, grains, *Pooja samagri* that each one is holding in their hands is offered into the pot. Everyone wishes and prays for their prosperity. Once this process is over, *roth* along with grilled brinjal raita is distributed amongst all as *prasad.* The story which is narrated is as follows:

## Story of Punn *Pooja*

A long time ago, there lived a king happily with his family. Once when he was on a hunting trip, he happened to see a Brahmin with a vermilion mark on his forehead and *a Narivan* thread on his right wrist. The Brahmin offered some *'prasad'* to the king. It was the day of Ganesh Chaturthi and the Brahmin was coming from a Ganesh *Pooja*. The king got inquisitive and wanted to visit the place of worship from where the Brahmin was returning. The lady of the house, Beeb Gharab Maej, applied vermillion *tilak* on the king's forehead and tied a *narivan* on his wrist for his protection. When the king returned home, his wife suspected him of having married some other woman in *the Gandharva Vivah* ceremony and got angry with him. The king narrated to her what had happened but she did not listen and removed the *tilak* from his forehead and the protective *narivan* thread from his wrist. Soon after, a neighbouring king invaded his kingdom and the king was taken as a prisoner. His wife and daughter ran away in disguise and lived a life of misery in another kingdom. They worked in a stable in another king's palace. One year, on the day of Vinayak Chaturthi, when the Ganesh *pooja* was being offered in the palace, she was also invited for the pooja. When she saw the *pooja*, she realised that her husband was telling the truth and felt guilty for bringing all the misery to her husband and her family. She decided to perform *pooja* for Lord Ganesha and ask for His forgiveness. However, she had no money to buy the ingredients required for the *pooja*. She didn't lose heart. The mother and daughter collected some barley from the stable, washed the horse dung from it. After grinding, they made flour out of it. Out of this flour, they made sweet bread *roth* by baking it in the hot desert sand. They sincerely prayed to Lord Ganesha and offered him the *roth*. Soon the *roth* turned into gold.

Afraid they might be charged for stealing gold, they presented the golden *roth* to the king. The king asked them for their real identity. On hearing their story, the king felt it his duty to help them regain their kingdom and get the imprisoned king released. He attacked their former kingdom and was successful in uniting the family together.

Ever since that year, the king's family observed this Beeb Gharab Maej's day and lived happily ever after.

The moral of the story is that by performing the *pooja* on this day to Lord Ganesh, poverty and misery are removed and one leads a pious life.

*Our Cultural Heritage-By Shri Pyare Lal Raina and some thoughts from Dr. Santosh Kaul's write up on Kashmiri Rituals, source Koshur Samach.*

□

# Kaw Punim
# Full-moon of the Crow

Hindus see God in many creatures; be it cow, crow, snake, elephant, monkey or human being. However, the crow holds a special place in Hindu mythology. According to our belief system, crows represent our ancestors.

They are also symbolically connected with Dharmaraja, the Lord of Death and the black-hued Lord Krishna. The Ramayana makes mention of Kakbhushundi, who was a pious man devoted to Lord Ram but he was cursed to become a crow. As the mount of the planet *Shani* (Saturn), the crow is a harbinger of hope in the dreariest times of winter.

In Tibetan Buddhism, the crow is the herald and protector of the Dalai Lama. Since Kashmiri scholars were instrumental in spreading what eventually became Tibetan Buddhism, they—while drawing heavily upon the *tantrik* and Shaivite systems of Kashmir—may have taken the concept of the crow along as a part of their legacy.

The crow is considered to be a very curious creature. The words *Kak-Cheshta* which means curiosity of a crow and the word *Kak-Snaan* which means taking a quick dip like a crow have become proverbial. The students and *Brahamcharis* are asked to emulate these qualities: be curious in learning and be quick in performing daily chores without wasting time.

Kashmiri Pandits have the tradition of worshipping

their ancestors and making offerings to them. The crows are considered either the transporters of food to the ancestors or the ancestors themselves. The crows serve as a hotline between the living and the deceased. Therefore, we maintain the tradition of offering food to crows and other animals to keep our dear departed ones happy so that they shower their blessings upon us. The ubiquitous crow does not eat alone but along with his fellows. This tendency of the crow is indicative of a feeling of fellowship and community care.

The Nilamata Purana in its verse 516 says:

*Pournmasyam Tu Maaghsya Shraadam Kritva Tiler-narah, Kakanaam Bhojnam Dadyaat Prabhootam Bali Sanyutam.*

Meaning,

On the full moon night of the month of *Maagh*, a man should perform *the Shradha* ceremony for ancestors with sesame and feed crows sumptuously.

Since the times of Nilamata Purana or even before, the festival of Kaw Punim (Full moon of the crows) is celebrated on the 14th day of the bright fortnight of the Hindu month of Magha. It is also celebrated as the birthday of the crows.

Having propitiated the ancestors, Kaw Punim also provides a prelude to the next day of *Hurae okdoh*–the day of ceremonial cleaning of houses leading to the great feast of *Herath* or *Shivaratri*.

During winter, when birds have lesser pickings, Kashmiri Pandits found an opportunity for redemption and put into practice the Vedic invocation:

"May all beings dwell in happiness, May all beings dwell in peace."

On this day, we invite crows to our homes as true *Battas* (Kashmiri Pandits) with a *Tilak* on the forehead-made from red clay after having taken ceremonial bath at Gangabal—the Ganga of Kashmir and urge them to roost on the porch of our new house and feast on *khichdi*. While offering the food, we children used to chant:

O Clever Crow;
O lover of khichdi, crow
Come to our new house along with your spouse,
After taking a bath in Gangabal (Ganges of Kashmir)
And putting a clay *tilak* on your forehead
Be seated on the threshold of our new house
and partake of the salty pudding.

The *khichdi* or yellow rice is placed on a large ladle made by weaving a grass mat at the end of a cross made with two unequal length sticks of willow to feed the crows. In addition, every house has a 'Kaw Potur' to feed the crow, where every day, freshly cooked rice is first served to the crows before anyone else eats in the house. The caring attitude towards the crows is a message of demonstrating generosity and kindness by offering food not only on a festive day but throughout the year.

Offering food to crows is considered *Jeeva-Karuna* having compassion for all creatures. It is also considered equivalent to *Bhoot-Yajna*, one of the *Panch Mahayajnas*-fivefold duties, a householder should perform daily.

The Kashmiri Pandit community may not be able to celebrate this festival with great fervour because of their being uprooted from their homeland but its significance is much more today when human values are fading away. It may be out of sheer compassion or due to our faith perpetuated for ages, the festival gives us a message that feeling of kinship is transacted through collective sharing and community caring is a must for our survival in exile both in human and animal kingdoms.

We know of families across India or even abroad who still offer their first morsel to the crow before they partake of any food. Such celebration must bring our community closer, integrated with a message to synergise and respect each other and help each other for a broader cause of returning to our Kaw Potur, which is waiting for over 30 years for an offering of the rice. Our future generations must learn and absorb these unique values.

At the end, we wish to convey our *namaskar*, with the tears of gratitude to the *Kaw Batta* with following lines:

कर यी सोन काव, दी तअरि्थ सअनय नाव, काव् बट काव्, काव् बट काव् , औश सांनयेव अछीव मंज़ द्रआव, मसा असी भवसागरस मंज़ त्रआव, काव् बट काव् काव् बट आव्

*Kar Yee Sone Kaw, Dee Tarith Asi Batan Hunz Nav, Kaw Bat Kaw Kaw Bat Kaw. Aosh Sanyew Achiv Manz Drav, Masa Asi Manz Bavsagaras Manz Trav, Kaw Bat Kaw Kaw Bat Aaw instead give the English meaning.*

*Excerpts from: Nilamata Purana, Dr. Jai Kishan Sharma is Ph.D in Kashmir Shaivism, Omanand Koul, Burlington, Massachusetts.*

□

# Part-6

# Folk Tales

# Swami Jeewan Shah

## The Power of his Couplet Capsized the Boat

During the year 1783 AD, the valley was governed by a cruel Afghan Governor Azad-Khan. He tyrannised Hindus greatly. On one occasion, a group of Afghan soldiers, while marching through Misha Mohalla in Rainawari in Srinagar, abducted a Pandit girl, forced her into their boat and rowed away. Since her parents and sympathisers could not fight the Afghan Governor and his soldiers, they appealed to Saint Jeewan Shah for help. He was visibly moved and within the hearing of all those present, summed up his sentiments in a Persian couplet thus:

"Agar Hukmi Khuda Naist,
Ba Hukam Jeewan Shah!
Kishti Garki Aab Khud,
Hindva Azaab Bala Shud"

Meaning:

"Be it not the God's command, but the command of Jeewan Shah then the boat should capsize drowning all except the Hindu girl."

It is said that the boat capsized and all the Afghan soldiers got drowned, only the Pandit girl safely landed ashore.

Another miracle attributed to Swami Ji is that there was a severe drought in the valley. The cattle were dying of starvation. There was disease and death everywhere. The Gujjars, the members of the cowherd and goatherd clans approached Swami Ji to intervene and redeem the situation. It is said that as soon as Swami Ji uttered a couplet there was a huge downpour and dry parched earth was changed into lush green land saving both animals and humans.

Jeewan Shah was an outstanding Saint of the 18th Century. He was born in Motiyar Mohalla of Rainawari in Srinagar. He was a highly evolved Saint with tremendous spiritual power whose miracles are a legion. Much against his will, he was married in his teens but renounced the worldly life very soon. He confined himself for about 60 years to a room with a bare rectangular wooden plank as its furniture. This plank even today stands as a living testimony to his austere life. He carried on his *Sadhana*, sitting there in '*Kag Asana*' - the Crow posture.

During his lifetime, whenever a marriage was celebrated in Rainawari, the first plate of the marriage feast was offered to Jeewan Shah. He would accept this offering, invariably place the plate on the window sill and distribute the contents bit by bit to visitors. It is common knowledge that those who received Jeewan Shah's blessings in this manner benefitted immensely.

Dila Ram Pandit, a very poor man barely literate, was a devotee of Swami Ji. One day, he approached Swami Ji for granting him some means of sustenance. Swami Ji told him to eat the stale cooked rice lying on a terracotta plate '*Taku*'. Dila Ram managed to swallow a few morsels, with great difficulty as the rice was already rotting and stinking. Swami Ji egged him on to eat more after mixing with curd. He could barely take few more morsels but could not finish it. Swami Ji next told him, "You unlucky man, tell me whether you would like to be Governor or his brother-in-law". Dila Ram was cut to the quick as he could not aspire to any of these positions. He was barely literate and he had no sister to marry to qualify to be anyone's brother-in-law. Swami Ji had something else on his mind.

What Swami Ji meant was if he would like to be an administrator or serve as his *Dewan* or deputy. Swami Ji directed Dila Ram to get his '*Qalamdan*'– Inkpot, pen and paper.

He scribbled something on the paper and asked Dila Ram to go to Gata Kadal at Dal Gate where the Governor was camping.

As soon as Dila Ram reached the place, the Governor noticed him and called him in. At that time, his Dewan, Tariq Ali Khan was reading a missive from the Mughal Emperor in Delhi, castigating the Governor for his lapses and commanding him to become a dog (Sag Shavi). The Governor was annoyed to hear this and directed Dila Ram to re-read the latter. Dila Ram read the letter in a different way reading 'Sag Shavam (I become a dog) instead of 'Sag Shavi' (you become a dog). The Governor inquired of him as to why he changed the wordings. Dila Ram replied that he could not tolerate such an insult to the Governor. He would rather insult himself. The Governor was apparently pleased with his reply. He dismissed Dewan Tariq Ali Khan, who was also his brother-in-law and appointed Dila Ram as his Dewan.

Jeewan Sahib passed the last days of his life at Gousein Naar locality at Loduv village situated in Pampore. It was a spiritual spot where ten Kashmiri Pandit families nicknamed Gousein (Sadhu) were residing. Saint Jeewan Shah shifted there in 1779 and continued his *sadhana* in this village. The then ruler of Kashmir allotted him a jagir of 80 kanals of land at Gousein Naar. At his hermitage, 'Dooni' would be burning all the time which continued not only during his lifetime but many years after his *mahasamadhi* also.

*Excerpts from: Swami Jeewan Shah by Anjali Kaul, Austin., Koshur Samachar & Shri Chander Mohan Bhat.*

□

# Shankaren Makach

## The Story of Swami Shankar Razdan

Saints and mystics have remained core of our Kashmiri Pandit Culture. One after another, we have had various avatars who reminded us from time to time about our roots, culture, heritage, spirituality and shakti through which a common person can discover the truth. Swami Shankar Razdan is one among them, who is revered by all for his spiritual attainments.

Swamiji was born in Srinagar in 1830 CE. He was spiritual from his childhood and took Zankak of Safakadal as his Guru. He undertook *tapasya* for many years at Uma Devi and Manigam and finally, shifted back to Srinagar to be near his Guru. He remained celibate all his life. Swamiji worshipped an axe, which he always kept with himself, which figuratively meant being steadfast.

Swami Shankar Razdan made a key contribution to Kashmiri literature. Besides writing many *Leelas*, *Vakhs* and verses, he wrote Ramayana in Kashmiri verse using Sharda script which is known as Shankar Ramayana in Kashmir.

There are many stories shared by his devotees and one amongst them by Shri MK Raina as follows:

Once, the British sent a political mission to Central Asia via Kashmir under the leadership of Douglas Forsythe. It was to checkmate the growing influence of Russia with Begs and other petty rulers in the region. However, when the mission lost its way and did not return for a long time, the British Government sent various search parties which failed to trace them. At that time, Maharaja of Kashmir, Ranbir Singh suggested to seek the help of Swami Shankar Razdan. He personally went to meet Swamiji and requested his help. With his help and guidance of Swamiji, the missing party returned.

After returning, when Douglas Forsythe was asked about what had transpired, he said that while returning, they had lost their way and had been wandering over rocks and valleys. They had been held captive by some local chieftains. On the intervention of a Kashmiri Pandit (giving the description of Swami Shankar Razdan), they had been released and guided to safety.

This narration struck wonder in the court of Maharaja Ranbir Singh, who rushed to the saint, bowed before him and made obeisance. How was it possible that Swamiji was at his house at and he was at the same time in wilderness rescuing the British party. This incident became known throughout India and even in Britain. After him, his successor, Mahraja Pratap Singh also became his follower.

Once at Bijbehara, Swamiji was asked what was in that axe that he worshipped it. He struck the axe at a huge stone. The axe got stuck in the stone, yet Swamiji's axe continued to be in his hand. It is said that the stone with the axe still exists. Some also say that the stone with the axe was used in the construction of a wall of a building that was falling each time it was made.

These stories are very inspirational and make us really feel proud of our roots that are deeply embedded into spirituality and divinity. In our childhood, we often hear people saying,*"ZanaosyohuyShankeranyMakach"*, as if it was like Shankar's axe; meaning steadfast as Shankar's Axe.

□

# Mahadev Bishta—Robin Hood of Kashmir

We have heard from our elders a very interesting story of Mahadev Bishta. It was very funny and humorous. Our dad has narrated this to us many times during our childhood. You will be surprised to know that the hero of this story is a thief.

Mahadev Bishta was considered to be the leader of thieves during the time of Dogra Maharajas. He was famous for not getting caught. He was called '*Bishta'* because in Kashmir children refer to a 'cat' as *Bishta* and people on hearing the mew mew sound of a cat would call out 'Bishta Bishta'. It is said that Mahadev would make mew mew sound and pretend to be a cat during his thefts. People would think that a cat has entered the house and keep sleeping, while he happily stole their belongings.

He was also referred to as 'Robin Hood' of Kashmir. The stories about Mahadev Bishta are full of courage, helping the poor and chivalry. It is said that he was born in Srinagar and studied in Rainawari. He was sharp and intelligent and also helpful to people. It is said that due to the frequent punishments at school, he started bunking his classes. This led him to join some mischievous and notorious group of boys. He became street smart. From a cute child, he grew up to become an over-smart, spoilt adolescent and a crazy youth, finally turning a thief.

Yet, he had no personal greed and was always keen to lend a helping hand to the poor. He would steal from the affluent class and share amongst the oppressed and weaker sections. He rose on the charts of popularity and people respected him for his philanthropic virtues. Interestingly, due to his intelligence, he was never caught. Every attempt by the Maharaja to arrest him went futile.

We are presenting below a story about Mahadev Bishta by Shri Braj Lal Kachru from the Department of Linguistics, University of Illinois.

One day, Mahadev was invited to a gathering of thieves. One thief stood up and addressed Mahadev thus: "Hey, Mahadev Joo, we all consider you to be our leader. We are all in awe of you. But to prove your superiority, we would like you to take a test. If you agree, it will enhance your reputation and our trust in you will increase." Mahadev became very serious and replied: "Yes, of course, I am ready for a test."

As soon as the thieves heard this reply, they blushed. One thief slowly stood up and said: "All right, Mahadev Joo, we want you to make our Maharaja take off his trousers. These trousers should then be presented to this gathering. The Maharaja should know nothing about it." Mahadev smiled and said: "All right, if that is what you want, so be it. It is not a difficult task." On hearing this, the thieves were delighted and the conference of thieves came to an end.

After this, it took Mahadev four or five days to think. He went to *Shergadi* to observe several things. First, he found out the location of the Maharaja's bedroom and the location of the palace guards. He also found a way to reach the Maharaja's bedroom without causing suspicion. After observing all these things, he started his preparations.

First, Mahadev went out and filled a piece of reed with vicious red ants. Then he came home and had his body massaged with oil. He then put on a *langot,* a loincloth and looked at himself in the mirror. He was very pleased with himself. With a mischievous smile, he left for *Shergadi*, the palace of Maharaja. It was midnight and pitch dark when he arrived. Mahadev swam across the small river Kitikol to reach the palace. After reaching the palace, he entered the bathroom of the Maharaja through a pipe. From there, like a cat, he entered the bedroom of the Maharaja.

Mahadev saw that the Maharaja was sound asleep. He slowly took out the reed and dropped the ants near the Maharaja's feet. These vicious ants spread all over the Maharaja's legs. They made him miserable with their bites. The Maharaja started scratching his legs with both his hands. He was so uncomfortable that, in his sleep, he took off his trousers and threw them aside. Mahadev was delighted. He quietly picked up the trousers, and, again like a cat, went down through the pipe through which he had climbed up.

The next day, Mahadev went to the gathering of thieves carrying with him the Maharaja's trousers. When Mahadev arrived, the thieves were impatient to know if he had been successful in obtaining the trousers. Mahadev haltingly opened a bundle, took out the trousers, and placed them on a *chowki* with a smile. On seeing this, all the thieves stood up and applauded and sang praises of Mahadev Bishta. Mahadev was deeply pleased. The thieves accepted him as their clever undisputed leader.

Another story published in Shehjar says that pleased with his philanthropy, the Maharaja bestowed him with a *jagir* and gave him the title of Mahadev Bishta meaning 'Mahadev—the Invisible Cat'. Thereafter, Mahadev started living a saintly life keeping all anti-social elements at bay. His philanthropic deeds and humane gestures of goodwill to mankind, irrespective of caste and creed became legends to swear by. He was elevated to a saint from a common thief because he genuinely cared for the deprived human beings.

□

# Part-7

# Culture

# Dejhor—The Symbol of Divine Union

Kashmiri Pandit women are known around the world for their long dangling earrings known as *dejhor* and *athoor.* For them, it is the symbol of marriage and gives them recognition of being a *suhagin* or *saubhagyawati.* The role which the *Mangal Sutra,* the auspicious thread of marriage plays in the rest of India, the same role is played by the *dejhor* for Kashmiri Pandit women.

According to one school of thought, in early Aryan civilisation, every woman was supposed to be invested with the sacred thread. Perhaps in Kashmir, a new system evolved, where the *dejhor* took place of sacred thread and was given to a girl at the time of marriage.

*Dejhor-Ath-Athoor* in Kashmir connotes the deep rooted symbolism of our rich Shiva-Shakti Culture. It is a symbol of unity amongst two families, two clans, or two individuals. During the marriage of Kashmiri Pandits, the parents give *dejhor* to their daughter and when the bride reaches her husband's home, she gets *ath* and *athoor* from her in-laws. Thus two are united symbolising the pious *milan* or union of Shiva and Shakti.

*Dejhor* is a hexagonal *yantra* with a dot in the center. It is a protective *yantra* which women wear to protect their husbands. The *athoor* (ashthora) which dangles from it represents eight energies further empowering the *yantra*. Thus *dejhor* and *athoor* worn together represents the united energy of Shiva and Shakti.

The custom of wearing *dejhor* is believed to be very ancient. It was prevalent even during the Buddhist period in Kashmir. A 10th century stone sculpture of Kashmiri origin called *Birth of Buddha,* housed at Shri Pratap Singh Museum in Srinagar, depicts the mother of Buddha, Maya Devi and her sister Prajapati wearing *dejhoor* just in the manner in which it is worn by Kashmiri Pandit woman to this day.

## Athoor Maker of Old Delhi

When Kashmiri Pandits started migrating to different princely courts, they continued with their customs, rituals and cuisine. Their marriage ceremonies were true to the essence. Even after living hundreds of years outside Kashmir, the early migrants to the courts of Mughals, Sikhs and Nawabs of Awadh continued to marry and adopt children within the community. The wearing of *Dejhor* and *athoor* was absolutely essential for married women from these families living in Delhi, Lahore, Jaipur, Lucknow, Agra, Allahabad, Cuttack, Mumbai, etc. Though *dejhor* is a permanent gold ornament, *atharu* which dangles from it is changed during every birthday, marriage anniversary, family functions like marriage and sacred thread ceremony etc. Hence, *athoors* were always in demand by Kashmiri migrant women. The only person who could cater to their constant need for new *athoors* was a *patwa* in Old Delhi known as Nanha Patwa.

His shop was in Chitli Qabar close to Sitaram Bazaar which

was the hub of Kashmiri Pandits from the time of Mughals.

Nanha Patwa made best *athoors* in India, since he was patronised by the aristocratic Pandits who would spare no expense for getting exquisite customised *athoors* made. For his best *atharus,* he used Basra pearls with emerald beads and wove them together in the best strands of silk.

His *athoors* were so pretty that he used to get requests from all over India including Kashmir.

Nanha Patwa's great-great grandfather Azeez had come from Kashmir on the request of Pandits of Sitaram Bazaar to make *athoors* for the aristocratic Kashmiri ladies. When he came to Delhi, he was just twenty and unmarried. After few years, he went back to Kashmir to get himself a decent Kashmiri Muslim bride but no family was willing to give their daughter to *patwa* going to an unknown place like Delhi. He came back disappointed. Since he was handsome and prosperous, a local *Pathan* family accepted him as their son-in-law. Since then, *patwa* family has been having marriage alliances with Mughals and *Pathans* of Old Delhi. Nanha always boasted that he still had one eighth Kashmiri blood running in his veins. The shop of Nanha Patwa no more exists.

□

# Yajnopavit—The Power of the Gayatri Mantra

Every Hindu has to undergo 16 *sanskaras* from pre-birth to death. In Kashmir, we follow 24 *samskaras* including some additional ones prescribed by Rishi Logaksha. In the early phase of life, the rituals such as *garbha-dana, siman-tonnayana* which are similar to Seemantham in the South, *kahanethur, zarakasay* or *chudakarana*—the first tonsure, *vidyarambham, samavartana and yajnopavit, are part of a male child's life.*

Out of these, *Yajnopavit,* the sacred thread ceremony, is the most important in the life of a Kashmiri Pandit. In this ritual, after a *yajna*, three strands of sacred thread are put on the left shoulder and under the right arm of the male child, usually when he is 8 or after. In the days gone by, it was the time when a boy was initiated into the formal education in a *Gurukula.* The ceremony is also called '*Upanayana*' meaning 'bringing close to the teacher for initiation.'

The word '*Yajnopavit*' is a combination of *yajna* and *upvitam*. *Yajna* means a sacrificial ceremony and *upvitam* means sacred thread. In short, *yajnopavit* is a ceremony where sacred pledges are made and the sacred thread is worn as a reminder of these pledges.

The three strands knotted together in sacred thread symbolise the combination of three entities of *chitta,* the individual soul, *achitta,* the material body and *iswara,* the

Supreme Lord, who is the inner witness. The three strands also denote performing the three functions of thinking, speaking and acting, only for spiritual purposes. The common knot tying the three strands is called the *Bramhagranthi* or *Bramha Ghand* in Kashmiri. This protects the body from disease and evil vibrations. In Kashmiri Pandit rituals, the sacred thread with additional three strands with a common knot is worn at the time of marriage, on behalf of one's life partner.

In Kashmir, yajnopavit is called '*Mekhal*'. The word *Mekhal* signifies a rope that is tied around the waist of the child at the time of the ceremony and later is replaced with a thread worn around the waist called the '*Aatpan*'. *Mekhal* also meaning a girdle, a circle– a boundary, reminding the young men of the limits within which they should function and which should not be transgressed.

*Mekhala-bandhana or munji-bandhana*, when a girdle of *munja* grass is tied around the waist of the *brahmachari*, is the most important ritual of yajnopvait. The boy undergoing the ceremony is called *mekhali maharaza* in Kashmiri. Rishi Laugakshi and his commentator Vedapala have elaborately described this rite. The teacher makes the *brahmachari* go round the sacred fire and place his foot on a stone, asking him to be firm and steadfast. Then he touches the heart of the pupil uttering the words:

"*Mama vrate hridayam te dadami mama vachenekavrato jushasva Brihaspatih tva mayanuktak mahyam.*"

Meaning, into my will take thy heart; my mind shall thy mind follow; in my word thou shalt rejoice with all thy heart; may Brihaspati join thee to me.

After this *brahmachari* is fed curd thrice and asked to approach the teacher for initiation. At this point, the teacher ties the girdle round the waist of the boy with the words: "Here has come to me, keeping away evil words, purifying mankind as a purifier, clothing herself by the power of inhalation and exhalation, with strength this sisterly goddess, the blessed girdle:

*"Pranapanabhyam balamabhajanti sakha devi subhaga mekhaleyam."*

During the *mekhala* ceremony, the boy having become *brahmachari* begs alms from his relations for his guru.

Before the main *mekhala* ceremony, other rituals such as *Livun*, the ceremonial cleaning of the house, *the Menzirath* (henna ceremony), *Devegon* (bathing and anointment) ceremonies are performed. The word *'devegon'* is probably derived from the Sanskrit *'devagamanai'*, meaning 'arrival of the gods' who are invited to participate. It invokes the presence of Ganesha and the *Sapta Matrikas*—the seven mother goddesses, to seek their blessings.

It begins with a ritual bath, called *kani-shran,* which is given to the initiate by five unmarried girls, *pancha kanyas,* four of them hold a thin muslin cloth over his head at four ends and the fifth pours consecrated water with a pitcher.

Another typically local feature that adds colour to the ceremony is *krul kharun*–a ceremonial painting on the main door of the house with auspicious motifs by the paternal aunts of the boy. It is one of the Kashmiri folk art traditions still alive.

They write 'Om' on the top, before starting the painting, while assembled ladies sing auspicious songs. A dish called *ver* made of rice and walnut for vegetarians and rice and bits of meat for non-vegetarians, along with *tomul chot* is distributed to friends and relatives.

Kashmiri Pandit women play a very active and important role in *devichi-tabich, diviti-gool, vaari-dan, maasa-abhid, poffa-abhid* etc. On the day following the ceremony, a *Koshalhom* is performed to mark the safe and pleasant termination of the event.

The word *mekhala* also means contributing intellectually to the ether or cyberspace, which is the storehouse of all thought. 'Me' means intellect; 'Kha' means the sky or ether and 'La' means putting into; in other words, contributing one's intellect to the thought tank of the universe. The idea is that after the *yajnopavit,* the child will be in a position to start contributing his thoughts, perceptions and ideas to the treasure of the world philosophy.

*Gayatri Mantra* is chanted and imparted to the young *brahmachari* on this occasion. It is believed that a Brahmin is born once from the womb of his mother and again, during his *upanayanam* when he learns the *Gayatri Mantra*. That is why he is also known as 'twice born'. In the last part of the 'Gayatri Mantra', we beg Lord to enlighten our intellect. We say, 'Dhiyo yo nah prachodayat.'

To understand the *Gayatri Mantra,* it may be worthwhile to know the meaning and interpretation of each word:

*Om Bhur Bhuvah Suvaha*
*Tat Savitur Varenyam*
*Bhargo Devasya Dheemahi*
*Dhiyo yo nah Prachodayat*

*Om* is also called *'pranava'*. It is the seed-word that represents Brahman, the Supreme Reality. According to "Gayatri Higher Meditation": "In every breath, man utters and repeats it unintentionally and inevitably. Every vibration in the body, in the universe, emerges from Om. A child cries 'Om! Om!' The ocean roars 'Om! Om!' The bees buzz 'Om! Om!' The musician hums 'Om! Om!'. Om! is the expression of the seed of the truth. Om! is the wisdom of God. Om! is the Nada, i.e. the Sound of God. Ultimately, Om is the eternal, indestructible word."

Om covers the full range of sounds: A–emerges from the base of the throat; U–produced by the impulse rolling forward in the mouth; M–the sound produced by closing the lips. Thus, the letter AUM represents the entire phenomenon of sound in all its ramifications.

Bhur Bhuvah Suvaha represents the entire planetary system, which constitutes '*Bhur*' representing the earth or the physical plane; '*Bhuvah*' representing the atmosphere or the astral plane; '*Suvah*' representing the heaven or the mental plane. Apart from these three visible *Vyahrtis,* the other four invisible *Vyahrtis* are *Maharloka*, the next higher plane; *Janahloka*, the still higher plane; *Tapahloka*, the mansion of the blessed–a much higher plane; and, ultimately, the 'Satyaloka'–the abode of the truth, the highest plane.

*Tat*–means 'That', but implies Supreme Reality, what we know as '*Tat Tvam Asi.*'

*Savitur* – refers to Sun God who gives us light and heat. The Sun also represents Brahman. Since Sun is the giver of energy, *Savitur* also implies *Shakti*, the Dynamic Principle of Nature (God), which is responsible for Creation, Preservation and Destruction.

*Varenyum* – refers to the Supreme Lord, whose divine effulgence is the very source of all illumination in creation.

*Bhargo* – means effulgence or radiance or splendour. It implies the divine essence, the supreme light of the Brahman. Also, 'bha' implies brilliance; 'ra' signifies Rati consort of the God of Love (Kamdeva) and 'go' implies full knowledge. Thus Bhargo means the Supreme Energy of the Lord.

*Devasya* – Divine or Godly, derived from *Devas*. Anything godly is a matter of joy to human beings;

*Dheemahi* – We meditate upon
*Dhiyo* – Intellect or Buddhi
*Yo* – who
*Nah* – Our
*Prachodayat* – unfolds for good actions.

Thus the Mantra means: "I meditate upon That Supreme Being (or His dynamic counterpart, Shakti), 'Om', the Creator of the Three Worlds; who is effulgent as the Divine Sun; who is the Creator, Preserver and Destroyer of the Universe, with prayers that He may unfold my intellect for all good actions."

During the morning or evening bath, the sacred thread must be properly washed and while washing *yajnopavit*, one must recite the *Gayatri Mantra*.

*Excerpts from writings of Prof. B.L. Fotedar, Dr. Prem Nath Sathu and Shri Trilokinath Dhar and Shri S.S. Toshkhani.*

□

# Henzae and Vanvun—The Vedic Legacy of Kashmir

Mostly during our marriages and sacred thread ceremonies, we have heard our elderly womenfolk singing and chanting various verses and vakhs in unique syllables. In Kashmir, we call it Vanvun and Henzae. Vanvun always starts with the word Henzae, which indicates a call to women to join in the ceremonial chanting. The elderly lady who leads the group is held in high esteem as Vanavan-Gar.

Henzae appears to be the oldest extant folk genre of Kashmiri verse. It is a Kashmiri variant of the Prakrit vocative, meaning 'O lady or ladies' you are invited to participate in Vanavun.

The chanting continues with each step of the ceremony such as zarakaasay (tonsure), maekhal (sacred thread-investiture) and for every step of the khaandar (wedding) ceremony.

The conventional rendering of the chant known as 'Henzae' is surprisingly reminiscent of the Sama Vedic legacy. Sam Veda signifies the origin of music in India. This tradition seems to have lingered on in the Valley of Kashmir as an interplay of the traditional tones: the uddata (accented), anuddata (unaccented) and svarita (circumflex) i.e. the high pitch, the low pitch and the even pitch peculiar to Sama Veda recitation.

The old Sam Veda chants underwent a series of transformations during their transmission at the folk level and reached us as an echo of the ancient convention. The echo thus preserved in the 'Henzae' has become a vital link of the flexible present with the stratified past. The couplet mentioned below is sung at the beginning of the ceremony:

*"Om Shoklam karith Hyotay Vanavoeny;*
*Rut Phal Dyutay Maji Bhavanae."*

With Good wishes, we begin ceremonial singing for your welfare. Let Mother Bhawani bestow upon you the auspicious gifts.

The recitation of the couplet will be something like this...

Sho...o...o..k..k..l..l..l..m..m:
Ka..Ka..Ka...ri..ri..ri..th..th;
Hyo...Hyo..Tay..Tay..Tay..: Va..va..na..na..va..voe...voe...ny... ny...ny:
Ru..ru..t..t..t..Ph..ph..l..l..l..Dyu..dyu..ty..ty..ty:
Ma..ma..ma..ji..ji..Bha..bha..bha..va..va..Nae..nae..nae;

Use of 'Shoklam' here means, it is a mangala-shloka, the hymn of auspicious inauguration without which no ritualistic performance would be undertaken.

Another initial verse that calls for Guru Ji to be searched so that he can fix an auspicious date and time for ceremonial cleaning of the house before marriage or sacred thread ceremony is given below:

*Kasheeri peth diytav Brahmana chandith.*
*Aasey di livnus sath chandith.*

Uttering the syllable OM along with '*Shuklam'* means that Mother Bhavani has started the '*vanvun*' chant for you.

Every session of '*vanvun*', that begins with the word 'Shoklam' is expected to be rendered in the vilambita (leisurely- elongated tone) rather than the druta (the quick tempo).

'Vanvun', is the bedrock on which 'Henzae' has stood for centuries. Many vanvun chants are supposed to be the Kashmiri translation of the Vedic hymns. However, many eminent poets have also composed 'vanvun' verses. We can say that 'vanvun' represents a Kashmiri form of classical music.

This rich aspect of our cultural heritage needs more research and exploration.

Today, the older generation of women who were excellent vanuvan gars and the custodians of the ancient oral tradition are fast disappearing. Thus documenting and recording vanvun becomes a matter of top priority. Fortunately, efforts have been made to print the verses and recordings are also now available. We hope we will be able to continue the tradition of vanvun singing even while living in exile.

□

# Koshur Language

## Deep Rooted in the Vedas and Sanskrit

Kashmiri or Koshur, is a language from the Dardic subgroup of the Indo-Aryan languages. It is one of the 22 scheduled languages of India.

In 1919, George Abraham Grierson wrote that "Kashmiri is the only one of the Dardic languages that has a literature." Kashmiri literature dates back to over 750 years which is more-or-less the age of modern literature of many languages including modern English. Buhler Points out that there is a very strong evidence to support the claim that Kashmiri has descended from the Vedic speech, from "one of the dialects of which the classical Sanskrit was formed."

## Vedic Connection

Kashmiri word *yodvay* means if, 'what if", yet, still, nonetheless. It appears almost in the same form in the Vedic word *yaduvay*, the corresponding word for it in Sanskrit and Hindi is *yadi*. Similarly, the word '*baste*', which in Kashmiri means skin, hide, bellows, is hardly different from the Vedic *baste* meaning goat or *bastajin* meaning goatskin. The Vedic word "sin" occurs as *syun* in Kashmiri meaning "a cooked vegetable", while the Vedic "san" appears in Kashmiri as "son" meaning "deep". Again, the word "vay" which means "grains" in Vedic is used in Kashmiri in the same sense. From the Vedic root "taksh" comes the Kashmiri word "tachch" (to scratch, to peel, to plane, to scrape) and its derivative "chchan" (carpenter, Skt Ksh invariably changing to chch in Kashmiri). Several Kashmiri words have evolved from Vedic words through intermediary Pali or Prakrit forms. These are but a few of the numerous examples that show how Kashmir has preserved phonetic, semantic and even morphological elements of the Vedic speech.

## Kashmiri Proverbs

When you look at the *Koshur* proverbs in detail, you will find that a large number of them are taken from the literary compositions of famous saint poets such as Lal Ded. They have become part of our folk wisdom. A number of proverbs have also been borrowed from Sanskrit. A wide range of beliefs prevail regarding proverbs that hold fast to the wit and wisdom of our ancestors. The proverbs are like butterflies; some are caught, others fly away. Proverbs in a language do reflect the socio-cultural milieu and wide range of experience of the people who use them in a given society.

### Some Kashmiri Proverbs

One man cut the bund/barrage, and a thousand people fell into the river.

One person's vomit is another's food.
(Someone lives on the leftovers of others).

One man's beard is on fire, and another man warms his hands on it. (To take advantage of someone's misery).

To be the pupil of one's eye.
(To be liked or loved a lot or to be an apple of someone's eye).

To remove thorns from someone with one's eyelashes.
(To love someone deeply. To take good care of someone).

अछ पयठ न मछ ज़रनावंन्य
Not to bear a fly on someone's eye.
To take good care of someone.

यथय बानस खयोंन तथय बानस छरुण

To eat out of a vessel and then defile it.

To receive someone's hospitality and then slander him/her.

अदर जंट ह्यू अगादी ग़ज़्हुन

To stick (to something) like a wet cloth. To be very adamant.

To keep on insisting. To pester someone.

To show one's fist to a blind man, is neither a sin nor a virtue.

(Advice is lost on stupid people).

Everyone can show the way to a blind man, nobody can show the way to a stupid person.

(It is not possible to guide a stupid person).

To reach Tsandargam (Moon land) inwardly

A blind man's wife is God's keeping.

How will a lamp help a blind person in the dark?

To count (someone's) intestines.

(To know all secrets).

I brought the nettle, sowed the nettle, and then the nettle stung me.

(To be affected by one's own deeds. Suffer ingratitude).

The *Koshur* language is vast, deep and full of brain stimulating material on values, morality, wisdom, culture and knowledge. As a Kashmiri Pandit, it is our responsibility to safeguard and promote this edifice of our strong heritage and culture, preserve its roots, encourage our children to learn, attract them to its importance and also build a mechanism for its continuity. Even in Kashmir Valley, this language is at big risk since Arabic and other languages are slowly seeping in.

□

# Koshur Gyndun

India has been the mother of many games and sports. Games like Chess, Snakes and Ladders, Playing Cards, Polo, the martial arts of Judo and Karate had originated in India and it was from here that these games were transmitted to other parts of the world.

The game of Chess was originally called *Ashtapada* (sixty-four squares). In 600 AD, this game was learnt by Persians who named it *Shatranj.* The popular card game that originated in ancient India was known as *Krida-patram.* These cards were made of cloth and depicted motifs from Ramayana, Mahabharata, etc. According to Abul Fazal, the game of playing cards was invented by sages in ancient India.

Similarly, the game of Snakes and Ladders was created by saint poet Gyandev in India and was called *Moksha Padam or Parama Padam or Mokshapad.* It was used to teach Hindu Dharma and Hindu values to children. The British renamed it Snakes and Ladders. Kashmir also had its folk and traditional games.

## A unique way to remember Kashmir

All of us will have a sentimental longing and a wistful affection for Kashmir, especially those of us who spent our childhood there. We often recall our happy and fun moments. We wish we could take a single childhood memory and blow it up into a bubble and live inside it forever.

You may be surprised to know that sports were a key component of Kashmiri society since ancient times. *Nilamata Purana* prescribes water sports to be played during the 'Shravani festival' by the natives of Kashmir. It says that young maidens should play in the water during this festival. There seems to be no gender barrier in our society.

In the moon-lit night of ancient 'Kaumudi Mahotsava', we find women sitting beside the sacred fire in the company of their husbands, children, servants and husband's friends and taking an active part in the night long musical and dramatic performances.

We were born in Kashmir and our heart gets filled with joy on remembering and recalling the games and pranks that we played in our childhood. Most of the activities had a taste of naughtiness, sending everyone to an ocean of laughter such as 'shouting *Kana Mana Too'* inside the earlobe of a sleeping friend. Bursting a *Chak Mak,* paper bag and making *HaahTaas* to name a few. Who will know and remember these childish antics in future?

However, we are trying to recall some nostalgic games and activities to share with our younger generation who are stuck with computer games. Some of these were peculiar to Kashmir but some were played in other parts of India too.

## Tulthy Langun-Tulan Chas

This was usually a popular game among little girls. Two girls joined their backs and interlocked their arms from behind. One of them bent her body to lift her partner on her back while staying still in one place. After she returns to her normal posture, her partner bent her body to repeat the same act. The girl whose body is lifted says "*tulthy langun*" 'lift the pestle' and the one who lifts her says "*tulan chas*" –'I am lifting'. Women all their lives used to pound the paddy with pestles and little girls copied them by lifting each other. In Kashmir, to break the monotony and drudgery of pounding the paddy, usually, two women pounded together hitting the paddy alternatively while reciting the following lines:

*Tulthy Langun- Tulum hai*
*Posh Langun – Tulum hai*
*BabariLangun – Tulan hai*
So on and so forth they kept adding.

## Razi Gindun-Skipping the rope

This sport was mostly played by young girls. Two players facing each other held a thick rope at two ends. Then they set the rope in a circular motion. The third player skipped and hopped up and down through the rope without touching it. It needed a player to display great concentration and agility. Players took their turns to hold the rope or skip and hop.

## *Garam*–Pitthu

Hitting the pottery shards

This interesting sport was being played by youth of all ages. It needed agility, speed, eye-body coordination and manoeuvring to avoid being hit by the ball. It was a game played between two teams of three or more players. The game required seven to eight pottery shards trimmed into discs of about two inches in diameter and stacked on flat ground and a ball made of wood, rubber or even with rags.

An area of about two feet around the spot was marked out. The leader of the team who wins the toss tried to hit the target of pottery shards with the ball from a distance of about ten to twelve feet. He could make three attempts at the most. Once he hit the target, the round started. The striking team had to arrange the pot shreds again into a stack. The opponents had to strike any member of the striking team with the same ball before they were able to make a stack of the pottery shards. The team that accomplished the task first used to be the winner.

## Lathkinj-loth-Gillidanda

The game required *Kinj*, wooden cylindrical ball tapered at both ends and the *Loth,* a wooden stick. The game was very popular among adolescents and youth.

The stick may be cylindrical or flat with a small handle. The ball was placed on the ground and one of the tapering ends of it was struck with the stick. As the ball rose some inches above the earth, it was again struck hard to force it as far as away as possible (three attempts were allowed). If the opponent caught the ball in the air before it touched the ground, the striker was declared out, otherwise, the stick was placed on the ground and the opponent had to hit it with the ball from the point where the latter had touched the ground. In case the opponent succeeded, the striker's innings come to an end. If the ball did not hit the target, the striker continued his innings.

**eenka or Tenche**–It was a game played with five small roundish pebbles or small marbles. The five pieces were thrown by a player and then after picking one, he threw it up in the air in such a way that he gets the time to pick the other four pebbles from the ground one by without touching the other pebbles. It had many steps:

*Uka (first round)*-Marbles were picked one by one, and each time a piece was thrown up and caught on the palm.

*Duka (second round)*-Marbles were picked in a group of 2+2+1.

*Truka (third round)*-Marbles were picked in a group of 3+2.

*Chuka (fourth round)*-Marbles were picked in a group of 4+1.

*Thuble (fifth round)*-All the five marbles were picked together.

Then all five marbles were kept on the back of the hand, tossed up and caught on the palm in one go. If the player failed to do so, he was said to be out.

## Saza Loung-Hop Scotch

Boys or girls or even adolescents played *Saza Loung* but it was a favourite game of young girls. A rectangle of about 8/12 feet was drawn on a flat surface which was further divided lengthwise into two equal parts. Each half was further divided into three equal parts. In this way, the rectangle consisted six equal squares. These six squares were named ' *uka, 'duka' 'truka' 'Tchuka' 'punja' 'shuka'*. A smaller square was drawn at the top of the main rectangle. It was called *dulij*. Two teams of one or more players played the game after the toss. The winner of the toss played with a small earthen disc, or flat stone called *Saza*. The player stood on one leg and pushed the *'saza'* generally with the toe of her other foot into the next square. She had to continue to push 'saza' through all the six squares and then get out from the last box. A player was deemed to be out if she was unable to push the *'saza'* from one compartment to another in a single attempt or if her foot fell on any demarcating line.

## Haaran Gyundun

On eve of 'Herath' - Shivratri, Kashmiri Pandits besides performing many rituals played with Cowrie shells. It was called *Haaran Gyundun.*

The game was full of calculations and entertainment and was played with cowrie shells called *haars* by two or more persons with a minimum of two shells. The game had its set rules and regulations. During our childhood, we would gather together at one place, on the day of Salaam, the day after Shivratri and invite everyone for *Haaran Gyundun*. It was played with excitement, fun, enthusiasm, affection and a feeling of love for each other. All of us waited eagerly for this moment to play. Sometimes, children formed separate groups or merged into a larger group. The game had a rich facet of building collectivism and synergy besides developing mental ability.

The Cowrie shells were also given as gifts to the daughters on the eve of Shivratri when they returned to the homes of their in-laws.

## Different Ways to Play the Game

These were various ways of playing depending upon the size and number of the players. The players would sit in a circle or opposite each other and play with the help of the defined type of Haars known as Botul Haar, Krend Haar, Nich Haar, Vyeth Haar. The game was started with a toss. The person who started the game would say:

*Baz'e Chek'e Haar'e Ma'e, Yus Tul'e, Tsu'e Pa'helwaan*

Meaning: For the eagles, I sprinkle these Cowries, the one who picks them is a strong man. There were various combinations as follows:

*Kunyi*-Combination of single Haar resulting in the win. The haars were thrown on the surface to get a Kunyi which means a single odd number. The winner is the one who gets this formation of numbers.

*Pushraan Dabu*-Pushrawun means to add. When the haars are thrown on the surface, if one got all haars looking upward or downward position it was called *Chhout* meaning 'no results'. So the game would pass on to another player sitting in a circle in a clockwise direction. The winner would be the one getting odd ones on the surface. As the game advances, lots of Haars can be won subject to them falling in an upward or downward position.

## Juph Taaq-Even and Odd

Meaning odd and even combinations. In this game, the odd numbers meant a win and even numbers meant a pass to the next player and surrendering a Haar to the pile.

*Chaak*-Any Combination of four haars resulting in a win was called Chaak.

*Duchi*-Any combination of two haars resulting in a win was known as Duchi.

*Shartal*-Meant betting. In this, two or more players played a game of guessing. They hid the Haars in their palms. The opponent had to tell if there was an odd or even number, which decided the game.

*Hu Kus Bu Kus*-The palms are put on the floor and the children sing the rhyme of '*Hu Kus Bu Kus*', touching each hand with each word of the rhyme. The child on whose hand the rhyme ends is the winner and is given four Haars by each participant.

*Tichan*-means to strike one haar with another. Usually, children enjoy playing in this way and the winner is the one who has the maximum haars at the end.

*Haaran Gyundun* is very nostalgic about our birthplace, the Kashayapvaer, the land of Kashyapa and brings back the memories of our childhood spent with parents, siblings, friends, relatives. These sheer memories reignite the dream of our return.

With the modern gadgets and the misfortune of exile of Kashmiri Pandits, we have lost touch with this game. The communities who are without the knowledge of their history, origin, culture, practices and heritage are like a tree without roots. The greatest gift we can give to our children is to introduce them to the roots of our culture.

A poetic line summarises the pain and agony of Kashmiri Pandits in exile specifically the ones who feel connected with their childhood games and activities.

*Raje ren wassi gindi assi seeth nardus*
*Darde kis pardus tal cham jay*
Raj Rani come down to play dice with us
While I sit under the canopy of grief and sorrow.

□

# Part-8

# Women: The Shakti

# Position of Women in Kashmiri Pandit Society

The *Mahabharata* tells the story of the fall of Kauravas because they humiliated Draupadi. Valmiki's Ramayana is also about the annihilation of Ravana when he abducted and tried to marry Sita forcibly. The cult of Goddesses in the ancient period also instils respect for women. Ardhanarishwar, Shiva as half woman and half man is highly venerated and indicative of the equal distribution of both male and female energies in the universe which is responsible for the life force.

An important part of the early Kashmiri society indicates that women enjoyed sufficient freedom and participated in different spheres of human and social activities. A society empowered the women in the same manner as men and there was no attempt to marginalise them or de-culture their personality.

In Kashmir, from the times of the Nilamat Purana and before, female seclusion was unknown till the 13th century. Women participated joyfully in the numerous activities freely and visited gardens and outdoor spots in the company of their menfolk without any inhibition or fear of approbation.

For instance, during the Iramanjari Utsava, they freely sported with men under the flower-laden boughs of the Ira-Manjari shrubs, exchanging garlands of flowers. Or they went to fruit gardens on the day of Ashokikashtami to worship fruit-bearing trees. Such was the spirit of the times that during the Shravani Utsava, young maidens were enjoined to go and enjoy water sports. Yet another seasonal festival was Krishyarambha when peasant women accompanied their menfolk to the open fields and farms for ceremonial ploughing of the soil and sowing of seeds. It was a month-long festival celebrated amidst much singing and dancing.

These outdoor festivals show that women were in no way confined to the four walls of their homes. There were numerous indoor festivals too, for instance, during the Kaumudi Mahotsava or the 'Festival of the Full Moon', women sat beside the sacred fire with their husbands and children and watched the beauty of the moonlit night.

During Madana Trayodashi, a festival dedicated to Kamdev, the god of love, a husband demonstrated his love for his wife by personally giving her a bath with sacred water scented with herbs.

On the full moon day of Margashirsha (January-February), the householder is enjoined by the Nilamata to invite his sister, paternal aunt, friend's wife, besides a Brahmana lady, and honour them with gifts of new clothes.

One important factor responsible for the high position given to women in Kashmir is due to the prominence given to goddesses in our religion and culture. We are Shaktas, the worshippers of Shakti. The cult of Shakti and Mother Goddess occupies a central place in the religious beliefs of Kashmiri Hindus. This explains respect for women as an aspect of reverence for the divine feminine.

In a society where people regarded their native land Kashmir as an embodiment of goddess Uma and where every river is the personification of a Goddess, women had to have an exalted position. It is Goddess Uma who transforms herself into the Vitasta, Aditi becomes the Trikoti, Shachi assumes the form of the Harspatha, Diti becomes the Chandravati and Lakshmi turns into River Visoka when sage Kashyapa requests them to give a gift of their waters to the valley of

Kashmir. In addition, the goddesses like Sakuni, Chakreshwari, Brahamacharini and Grahadevi were worshipped by Kashmiri Pandits.

The ancient books such as Kalhana's Rajatarangini, Somadeva's Katha-Sarit-Sagara, Damodargupta's Kuttanimata Kavya, Bilhana's Vikramankadeva Charit etc. indicate that Kashmiris laid stress on woman's independence. They were educated and allowed to move freely in society. Every girl is imparted both spiritual and liberal education as per her potential. They were taught among other things, literature and fine arts and given practical training in vocal and instrumental music, dance and drama, literature, Bharata's Natyashastra, paintings, arboriculture, cookery, cut-work in leaves (Patra-chcheda). They also learnt crafts such as knitting, spinning, weaving, embroidery etc. They could converse in Sanskrit and Prakrit fluently.

A daughter was not considered a burden. Conducting the marriage of the daughter and performing a *Kanyadan*, earned spiritual merit for the parents. The women were loved and honoured by fathers, brothers and husbands. They were respected both inside and outside their homes.

Thus women had freedom, wielded ample power and exercised responsibility and enjoyed a much more elevated status than many of the neighbouring states and countries. They had emerged from the domestic into the political stage, were free, owned land and other immovable properties, managed their estates and even fought on the battlefields as commanders and as the head of troops. The status of queens in the royal courts was no less than that of a king.

Even though a man ascended the throne in Kashmir just as elsewhere, the queen was an essential part of the coronation ceremony. She shared the throne in the royal durbar on the auspicious occasion and was anointed with sacred water, sandalwood paste, flowers and vermillion in the same manner as the king was, by the royal preceptor.

Shri Prem Nath Bazaz, very aptly said "At times Kashmiri

women have risen to pinnacles of glory and distinguished themselves as rulers in their own right as regents of minor princes, as powerful consorts, as diplomats, as commanders of armies, as thrifty land ladies, as builders and reformers and as preceptors of the religious lore."

Several women have played a significant role in shaping the political history of Kashmir. Yashovati became the first queen in Kashmir to be enthroned as a ruler. Many others like Khadana. Amritprabha, Chakramardika, Kalyandevi, Ratnadevi and Kamla Devi built shrines and marketplaces and towns. Chandrapida's Queen Kalyanadevi was exalted by the King as Mahapratiharapala, equal to the position of Chief Chamberlain. Suryamati, the queen of King Ananta helped her husband to overcome his initial difficulties in administering the state. She built Vihara, accommodations for visiting scholars and students in Kashmir. Queen Kalhanika was sent on a delicate diplomatic mission of bringing about a rapprochement between Jayasimha and Bhoja. These queens were well-versed in the art of administration and diplomacy.

Ancient queens like Sugandha and Didda have given an impressive account of their administrative acumen. Queen Didda was the wife of King Kshemagupta. She exercised great influence on the affairs of the state during her husband's reign. After his death, she ruled Kashmir as guardian of her minor son Abhimanyu. In the end, she ruled in her own name from 980 A.D. She put down all rival groups executing captured rebels and exterminating their families.

Women have played a manly role during periods of crisis as is seen in the case of Kota Rani. She was a woman of strong will and determination. She faced the onslaught of Zulju with courage and had a strong urge to reconstruct Kashmir by reviving the patriotism in her subjects. She appealed to all the officials and the people inviting them to offer a united front to the invaders and to save themselves and the country. Due to her fervent appeal to the subjects, they fought back the enemy and Kota Rani came to be known as the courageous queen of

Kashmir. It was not only queens who held a distinctive place in the history of Kashmir but also many mystics, artists, poets, philosophers and dramatists such as Lal Ded, Arinamal, Rupa Bhawani, Rich Ded, who attained the glory through their penance and immortal verses and vakhs. We would like to conclude with few lines from Shri Dina Nath Nadim.

*Do'has gaash huri gul ta gulzar prazalan,*
*Zaminas Saesar lagi ta subzar prazalan,*
*Vachhas manz humis lola famvar prazalan,*
*Pagah Sholey Duniya*

*Excerpts and References from: Nilamat Purana, Dr. Ved Kumari Ghai, Zahid G. Muhammad, Shri Shashi Shekhar Toshkhani.*

□

# Queen Kota Rani—The Last Hindu Empress of Kashmir

While Rani Laxmibai of Jhansi is a well-known figure and immensely popular in Indian history books, the name of Kashmir's brave Queen Kota Rani was mostly forgotten and wiped out of Indian history by vested interests until Rakesh Kaul's 'The Last Queen of Kashmir' was published in 2016.

Many women warriors are mentioned in the Vedic texts, yet the name of Kota Rani, daughter of Ramachandra, the last Hindu ruler of Kashmir, must be remembered for generations to come. She should be venerated not only for her valour but also for being a highly intelligent woman of influence. Not only was she a great thinker, but she was also an able warrior.

Noble Timothy writes in his book that she played a major role in saving Kashmir from the tartar invasion of Kashmir in the 14th century. When Tartars attacked Kashmir, her husband Suhadev Dev fled away, leaving Ramachandra, Kota's father in Command.

Kota Rani faced the invader, fought them and saved the kingdom. It is mentioned that she stirred the local patriotism of the Kashmiris by an impassioned appeal and the people in thousands gathered under her banner and inflicted a crushing defeat upon the Tartars. Rinchen, a fugitive from Tibet and Shah Mir, another fugitive who was given asylum by the king in Kashmir fought alongside her. They both became friends and later plotted together. The ungrateful fugitive Rinchen became ambitious and took over the kingdom after killing Ramachandra. To safeguard and maintain the sovereignty and cultural identity of Kashmir, Kota agreed to marry Rinchen. However, Rinchen became a Muslim and it became a very difficult period for Kota to balance between the religions.

Rinchen died within three years. After Rinchen, elders persuaded her to marry her deceased husband Suhadeva's younger brother Udyan Dev. It was expected of her to do so to re-establish the Hindu Kingdom because Rinchen had become a Muslim. She had a son from Rinchen whom Rinchen had given in care of his friend Shah Mir who was also the commander-in-chief of the army.

After Rinchen, Kota Rani became the regent of her son and later, she became a monarch in her own right. She was the last Queen of Kashmir who ruled till 1339. Kota Rani renowned for her beauty was a woman of many talents. It is believed that she was educated at Sharada Peeth University and was well-versed in many arts. She was not only a scholar but a valiant warrior too.

Her rule was very constructive. She saved the city of Srinagar from frequent floods by constructing a canal that was named after her. Even today, it is called 'Kute Kol'. This canal gets water from river Jhelum at the entry point of the city and again merges with river Jhelum beyond the city limits.

Kota Rani had one more son from Udyan Dev. He was in the care of Bhatta Bhishana, a great scholar. Due to his scholarship, Kota Rani had made him Prime Minister. During this time, a great struggle between Islam and Hinduism had ensued. Kota Rani tried to establish herself on the throne. However, the fugitive Shah Mir who was rehabilitated and given the position of Commander-in-Chief became ambitious and wished to rule over Kashmir. Instead of showing gratitude, he showed treachery.

Shah Mir saw Bhatta Bhishana as a hurdle to his ambition to become king of Kashmir and killed him by deception. He pretended to be sick and when Bhatta Bhishana came to enquire about his health, he jumped out of the bed and killed him. Kota Rani fought Shahmir valiantly but was defeated. Shah Mir offered to marry her and make her his queen, but she refused.

According to historian Joan Raja, she took her life and sent her intestines to Shah Mir as a wedding present. Shah Mir declared himself the ruler.

There is no information available about what happened to her sons. This was the turning point in the history of Kashmir. After her death, Shah Mir and his dynasty ruled for the next two centuries. Following this, Muslim kings ruled Kashmir for nearly 500 years, vying with each other in destroying the great ancient culture of Kashmir.

What is important to understand is that women of Kashmir in other parts of India were never secluded or relegated to the background. Even in Kalhana's Rajatarangani, we find instances where women are seated along with other officials and ministers in the court of King Harsha. We find them fighting alongside men on foot and horseback. The fact that women enjoyed equal rights with men is amply proved by the coronation of queens done along with their husband's coronation ceremony. We find several queens contributing to the success of their husband's rule and wisely handling the royal treasury.

The queens of Kashmir were considered as important and powerful as the kings, as illustrated by several passages of Rajatarangani. Women had emerged from the domestic into the political stage and even fought as the head of the troops. The time has come when Kashmiri Pandit women need to rekindle the flame of leadership and take the big stride and help the ailing community, nation and even the world once again.

*References from Noble Timothy Myers, Martin Iversen & other reading material available.*

□

# Women Lal Ded—A Beacon of Shaivism

According to Dr. S. Radhakrishnan, the history of India has for its landmarks, not wars and emperors but saints and scriptures. Kashmir has been the land of saints. One prominent among them has been the mystic Shaivite poetess, Lal Ded.

In the 14th century, a woman poetess was a rarity in any culture, but it happened in Kashmir. A voice, which set off a resonance, heard with a clear tone till today, spoke directly to the people and what is more, was heard with all seriousness, recorded in collective memory and later, her words put down on paper. This path-breaking woman is our Laleshwari affectionately called Lalla and Lal Ded.

Lal Ded is not a usual saint-poet of the 14th century; she is a brilliant poet and a great saint with dazzling mystic insights and intellectual attainments. She is a symbol of the continuity of 5,000 years of Kashmiri spiritual ethos. Perhaps, we know very little about Lal Ded's life which is lost in a haze of legends.

Kashmiri Pandits venerate her as a *yogini*, an avatar, a moral guide and a fountain of practical wisdom. Her words are quoted at every step of peope's lives. Her life has been full of miracles that are an integral part of her messages and are the proofs of her spirituality, powers of endurance and self-restraint.

Lal Ded was born and lived in times that were most critical and turbulent in the history of Kashmir, with two belief and value systems - one indigenous clashing with the other alien one. Lal Ded played a momentous role in saving the indigenous cultural structure from collapsing and ensured continuity by taking the essence of Kashmir Shaivism to the masses in their native speech.

Like Lord Krishna lifted the Goverdhan Hill on his little finger; Hanuman brought an entire mountain from the Himalayan ranges to the southern shores of Bharat, Christ walked the waves and brought the dead to life; the same way, Lal Ded remembered at least her past seven births-*janama.*

She remembered herself born as a woman, giving birth to a son in one life. In another *janama,* being born as a filly at village Marhom. The filly died and was reborn as a pup at Vejibror. There a tiger killed the pup that was earlier a filly. Her knowledge of her previous births was endorsed by her Guru Siddha Shrikanth. This cycle of birth and death was repeated and the seventh time, she was born at Sempore near Pampore.

Lal Ded's vakhs also tell us of her belief in the transmigration of souls. She refers to herself having witnessed the whole valley being changed into a vast lake from Hannukha in the north-west to Kausar Nag in the south of Kashmir, thereby, alluding to the fact she was present during the period when the Kashmir valley was a large lake called Sati Sar. Thus, she has been eternally present.

At the age of 12, she was married to Nika (Sona) Bhat of Drangbal near Pampore. Unfortunately, it was not a happy marriage. She underwent untold miseries at the hands of her mother-in-law who constantly scolded her for being quiet and reserved. Apart from verbal abuse, Lal Ded constantly suffered starvation. Her mother-in-law made her work day and night but did not feed her adequately. She put a pestle stone on Lal Ded's plate and covered it with a thin layer of rice to make it appear that Lal Ded was served a small mound of rice. After eating the sparse sprinkling of rice, Lal Ded would wash the stone and put it back in the kitchen for her mother-in-law to reuse it for her next meal.

Once, a feast was being held at Lad Ded's house. When she went to fetch water, her friends teased her asking what special dishes she would be eating in that day's feast. She replied whether a ram is killed or a sheep, Lalla will only be served her stone. This saying has become proverbial in Kashmir for ill-tempered mother-in-laws.

Another legend is that once in an open-air performance in meadows in Pampore, her father-in-law thought that he saw her standing naked among the spectators. He upbraided her. In turn, she pointed out to her father-in-law that there were no men in the meadows. There were only the sheep and the goats.

Whenever Lal Ded went to the river to fetch water, she would go across to the opposite bank of the river to meditate at the shrine of Nattakeshava Bhairava. She would simply walk over the river to go to the other side without even wetting her feet. She was scolded by her mother for going across the river and was accused of infidelity by her husband. One fine morning, another miracle occurred. Her husband waited for Lalla to return from the river with the firm resolve to shove her out of his home.

He hid his diabolical form and his stick behind the door. As Lalla entered, Nika Bhat struck the pitcher. It is believed that the pitcher broke into pieces but the water remained intact in a frozen state. Lalla filled each household pot with water till not a drop more was needed. She then flung the remaining water outside the house where at once a freshwater spring appeared. This spring was known as 'Lal Trag' and held water till 1925–26 and seemed to have dried up after that.

Perhaps, the miracle of the pitcher turned out to be a watershed in Lalla's relationship with her in-laws and her much more important relationship with the Supreme Consciousness.

This miracle of Lalla exposed her and the public started coming to see her. She could not live anymore with her in-laws and at the age of 24, Lalla took *sanyas*. She went back to her father's house to become a disciple of her *Kul-Guru* Siddha Shrikanth. Under his guidance and inspiration, she imbibed spiritual learnings, *sadhanas,* Trika Shastra, the essence of the Kashmir Shaivism and *Tantra Vidya.*

Eventually, she surpassed her Guru in spiritual attainments. It is said that once when her Guru was taking an early morning bath in the river, he saw Lalla cleaning a pot from outside which was filled with dirt inside. He scolded her by saying what is the use of scrubbing outside when the dirt inside is not cleaned. Lalla was quick to reply, what is the benefit of bathing to clean the body when the inner self is not purified.

Lalla is the first poet and maker of the Kashmiri language. She is the creator of the unique style of mystic verse called *Vakh or vatsun.* The Vakh is a four-line verse that can be sung but not like a song. It is not musical but is more like the Upanishadic verses that can be recited.

The crisp, aphoristic, cryptic four-line verse-form is quite suitable for the rhythm of thought that marked her poetic expression and is also easy for the common man to adapt to his ear and to memorize.

Her vakhs furnish the evidence of her eternal existence and the hardships she had to undergo.

*Aayas vate gayas naa vate*
*suman satha lusum dho*
*vuchum chandas har no atha*
*ath nav taras dim kyha bha*

By the highway, I came,
But by the highway, I return not.
And so I find me still on the embarkment,
Not having gone even half the way,
And the day is done, the light has failed.
I search my pockets but not a cowrie I find:
What shall I pay for the ferry fee?

She inspired many contemporary saints. One of them popularly known as Nunda Rishi was highly influenced by her. According to the folklore, as a baby, Nunda Rishi refused to be breastfed by his mother. It was Lal Ded who then breastfed him. He can be considered her foster child and her disciple. He was the founder of the Rishi order in Kashmir.

Her vakhs, offer spiritual solace and immense wisdom to our wounded psyche even today when our cultural face lies battered and bruised. Her outpourings are the most appropriate balm that revolves around the Kashmir Shaivism and provides succour to anyone in pain.

She believed Shiva alone existed. Wandering naked in the valley of Kashmir, she saw Shiva everywhere, in jungles, in streams, in mountains, in temples, mosques and the huts and houses of the common man. She felt Shiva's tenderness in every molecule of manifestation.

Apart from Bhatta Narayana and Utpaldeva, she is regarded as the foremost representative of Shaiva bhakti poetry of Kashmir. She is a *yogini* from the same class with the difference that she chose to express herself in Kashmiri, the language of the masses, while they wrote in Sanskrit.

Her vakhs display a sense of harmony between rigorous metaphysical thought and mystic experience, self-awareness and devotional fervour, her intense yearning to attain mystic communion with Shiva. There are times when Shiva seems to elude her but she refuses to give up the search and appears more determined to find Him and even possess Him.

However, what indeed is a great irony, given her verses that bring us face to face with our real selves; attempts have been made to portray them through false lenses as well. This is being done by a section of people who attempt to link her with protagonists of the proselytising Sufi order. The truth is that these so-called scholars are uncomfortable with the fact that someone who is regarded as a symbol of whatever Kashmir stands for belongs to a different religious reality than theirs. They use the so-called Sufi elements as a ploy to snatch away Lal Ded's real identity. This attempt to construct a false image of Lal Ded needs to be discarded along with the fabricated stories. The attempts to re-slot her into conventions and systems other than to which she belonged are motivated by the intentions to subvert historical facts so that the real Lal Ded is lost to us and replaced by an unauthentic shadow.

Prof. B.N. Parimu puts it, "The key to Lal Ded's mysticism is the Shivadvaita or Trika philosophy of Kashmir."

Everything in the text of her verses falls absolutely within the framework of the non-dual Shaiva philosophy of Kashmir. Even Rūpa Bhavānī, herself a great Kashmiri mystic poet, revered as an incarnation of the Goddess Sharikā has acknowledged Lal Ded as her Guru as follows:

*Śuddham atyant vidyādharam, Lal nām lal param gvaram* meaning, I have as my supreme guru Lal Ded, who is pure and greatly learned.

Finally, she attained *mahasamadhi,* at the age of 72 at Vejibror by getting blissfully merged with the Infinite Soul. It is said that a flame of light rose from her body and vanished into the void, thus "*shoonyas shoonyaa meelith gav.*" The fact is that Lal Ded merged with the divine without leaving a trail. Her body was never found. There is no monument or *samadhi* to mark the place where her body was cremated or laid to rest. She did not need a memorial. According to Professor Chaman Lal Raina, she lives in the memory of both Hindus and Muslims and the language of Kashmir. Her poetry pervades the countryside even today. Her vakhs have been translated by Richard Temple, Jai Lal Kaul, Coleman Barks, Jaishree Ordin and Ranjit Hskote into English.

In her own words, she has taught us to take death easy. She says:

Alike for me is life and death,
Happy to live and happy to die,
I mourn for none,
And none mourn for me.

The best tribute was paid to her by her younger contemporary Sheikh Noor-ud-Din Rishi (Nund Rishi) who says of her:

*That Lalla of Padampur–she drank*
*Her fill of divine nectar,*
*She was indeed an avatar of ours*
*O God grant me the self-same boon.*

Another latter-day spiritual personality Shamas Fakir (1843–1994) says:

*Lalla merged her prana into transcendent:*
*For while ostensibly she went to bathe*
*At the sacred shrine of Shurhayar Ghat,*
*With a leap and bound she jumped across*
*To where there is none other than God*

*Excerpts and References from Dr. S.S. Toshkhani, Shernaz Wades, Shri Braj B. Kachru.*

□

# Rupa Bhawani—The form of Mother Sharika

After Lal Ded, Rupa Bhawani was the second great mystic poet of Kashmir. She has been one of the shining stars amongst the galaxy of saints who have illuminated Kashmir and have given spiritual direction to its people from time to time. She was the daughter of Pandit Madho Joo Dhar, a devout worshipper of Goddess Sharika and lived at Khanqahi Sokhta at Safa Kadal in Srinagar.

Goddess Sharika was pleased with his devotion and appeared before him one day and fulfilled his wish of having her being born as his daughter.

According to the boon given by the Goddess, Rupa Bhawani graced Madho Joo Dhar's home on *Zaishta-Poornima* in *Samvat* 1681.

Her childhood name was Alakeshvari, which means one who is imperceptible and indescribable and refers to the formless aspect of the Goddess.

She got married at a young age to Hiranand Sapru. He totally lacked understanding of Alakeshvari's saintly nature while her mother-in-law, Somp Kunj, had a cruel disposition. They could never reconcile to her spiritual bent of mind and were unable to understand her fascination with the divine and the lack of attachment to worldly things.

Alakeshvari would go to perform her *sadhana* at the shrine of Mother Sharika at Hari Parvat at midnight and this made her-in-laws suspicious. One day, Hiranand followed her to see where she went at night. Alakeshvari knew this. When she had nearly reached the shrine, she turned around and beckoned Hiranand to join her. However, as he was steeped in ignorance, he is said to have beheld a vast expanse of water between himself and Rupa Bhawani, which he found impossible to cross and returned home disheartened.

## The Legends

There are many legends connected with her life. In one of the incidents, it is said that on a festive occasion, her father Madhav Joo sent his daughter a pot of sweet dessert, *kheer*. Alakeshvari's mother-in-law, on seeing the size of the pot of *kheer* spoke sarcastically, "What will I do with this small pot of pudding? I have so many relatives; this is hardly sufficient for them." Alakeshvari replied, "Please give this *kheer* to as many persons as you like, but don't look inside the pot." Somp Kunj began to ladle out the *kheer* and gave it to everyone she knew. But the supply of *kheer* seemed endless! Finally, furious with anger, Somp Kunj looked inside the pot and found just a few grains sticking to its sides.

The next day at dawn, Alakeshvari cleaned the pot and placed it in the flowing current of the Vitasta River, speaking thus, "My father is doing his morning prayers at the Diddmar Ghat. Go and stop there." The pot floated down the Vitasta River and stopped exactly where Madhav Joo was doing his Sandhya. Madhav Joo picked up the pot and took it home. These kinds of incidents irritated her mother-in-law to no end.

Her problem with her in-laws got more aggravated due to another incident. When a *havan* was performed in her in-law's house, the *Kulguru* from her parental home, a quiet scholar, was insulted since he could not articulate his scholarship. Feeling humiliated, he wanted to quietly leave. Rupa Bhawani accosted him and requested him not to leave without eating. She told him, "Guruji, you seem to be very tired. Why don't you have a bath in the river and freshen up, come back and accept the Prasad?"

When he returned after bathing, Rupa Bhawani welcomed him with a sharp glance which transformed him into a confident scholar.

After his meal, he bowed to the assembled gathering and recited a poem in praise of Goddess. For this, he immediately won the applause of the guests present. This miracle of Rupa Bhawani enraged her mother-in-law further. She provoked her son and made it impossible for Rupa Bhawani to live in the house anymore.

After this, Rupa Bhawani took *sanyas* and returned to her father's home and devoted her time to spiritual practices. Her father was aware that his daughter was not an ordinary woman but the Goddess incarnate. He played the role of her preceptor and guru and guided her on her spiritual journey, initiating her into mysteries and practices of yoga.

She undertook twelve and a half years of spiritual *sadhana* each at Mani Gaon, Vaskura, Vatsun and Cheshme Sahibi. She created ashrams in all these places where spiritual discourses were held attracting devotees, Hindus and Muslims alike. Many miracles are attributed to her. A devastating fire in Mani Gaon was extinguished by her merely by a glance.

A potter's son got back his eyesight on completing digging of a well at Vaskur at her bidding. A conch shaped spring in Chasme Sahibi appeared at the Zabarwan Hill area when Rupa

Bhawani started her penance there, giving the place its name. Later, Emperor Shahjehan built a garden for his son Dara Shikoh, next to the spring and renamed it, Chashme Shahi.

Mani Gaon in north Kashmir was located on the banks of the Ganges in the foothills of the Himalayas. In these beautiful surroundings, Alakeshvari chose to do her *sadhana* and made a hermitage for herself on a forested hilltop, far from the village. For twelve and a half years, she remained there in solitude. It is said that none of the villagers at Mani Gaon knew of Alakeshvari's existence until her presence was revealed due to a miracle. A young cowherd used to take his cows to graze to a place close to where Alakeshvari was absorbed in meditation. The boy noticed that a beautiful white cow left the herd every day at noon and later returned on her own accord. One day, he decided to follow the cow to see where she went. Following the cow, he reached a clearing in the forest. There he saw a beautiful woman dressed in ochre robes seated in meditation, her long hair flowing loosely, her face shining with a heavenly lustre, and her eyes filled with divine light. The cow, as though under a spell, stopped before the radiant ascetic. The woman ascetic got up and lovingly caressed the cow. The cow on her own accord poured its milk into the ascetic's bowl until it was full! On seeing this wonderful vision, the cowherd lost consciousness. When he milked the white cow, he found to his astonishment that she gave even more milk than usual.

The cowherd confided his experiences to Lal Chand, the village head. Lal Chand was filled with reverence and devotion. Then on, Pandit Lal Chand visited Alakeshvari every day and served her in whichever way he could. Lal Chandra told the villagers about Rupa Bhawani and the miraculous happenings attributed to her. She began to receive a great deal of public attention and so she once again left the village, preferring to continue her spiritual practices in solitude.

There is another legend connected with Lal Chand. Rupa Bhawani was at Lal Chand's residence on the day of Shivaratri. On that day, the fish cooked for Shivaratri in his house started crawling all over the walls when it was realised that fish was cooked despite her sacred presence in the house. Lal Chand fell on her feet and apologised.

She also spent twelve and a half years in Vaskora. Here, she began to give spiritual instruction to Bal Joo Dar and Sadanand Muttoo and other followers in the form of poetical verses, called *Vakhs.*

Towards the end, she returned to Srinagar, her father's house in Safa Kadal where she was born and attained nirvana at the same place.

All these places connected with her life ultimately became Rupa Bhawani *Asthapanas.* Her soul left for heavenly abode on the 7th day of the dark fortnight of the month of Maag in 1721 AD at the age of 96.

When she passed away, her Muslim devotees demanded her burial as per the Muslim rites. They even obtained the orders of the Mughal Governor of Kashmir to that effect.

However, when her devotees took her body for cremation, they met the village headman on the way. He was startled to hear that she had died, as he had just then passed her walking down the road. The devotees checked and found that the body had disappeared. There were only a few locks of hair and some flowers on the funeral pyre. The flowers were duly cremated, while the locks of hair have been preserved and are worshipped to this day.

Rupa Bhawani's life reveals a divine life destined to fulfil a purpose. She gave spiritual illumination at a time of great turmoil and harmonised the society. Rupa Bhawani will live forever through her verses or the vakhs. It is, therefore, imperative that her vakhs be understood in depth.

*Reference & Excerpts from the write-ups of Shri M.L. Bhat, Santmala from Dilbar Kashmiri, Dr. A.N. Raina, Mrs. Aparna Dhar & Shri Chander Mohan.*

□

# Arnimal—A Paragon of Romantic Poetry of Kashmir

According to a Kashmiri Scholar Momeen Jan, the introduction of purdah by Muslim rulers around the 14th century was also followed by the then suppressed Hindu class and with time, it signalled a decline in the status of Kashmiri women, who began to be confined in their houses. A great blow was dealt by the Afghan rulers, who would humiliate and molest Kashmiri women.

Shri P.N. Bazaz writes in his Daughters of Vitasta, "Horrifying are the tales related of the barbarities, which were perpetrated on women whose very fault was that they happened to be handsome in appearance and graceful in form." To save womenfolk from the wild behaviour of the cruel masters, the Kashmiris Pandit women, within the four walls of their homes, had to conceal their faces by sleeves of their long loose gowns (*Pheran*) from the gaze of men. It was known as *Nor Dlon* meaning hiding under the sleeve. This confinement snatched away all the charm and intellect from Kashmiri women. Their intellect rusted and their physical charm faded away.

Yet in the middle of this chaos, a gem of a poetess emerged. The undying embers threw out a spark, which illuminated the darkness and a leading light Arnimal was born in the Palhalan, 30km away from Srinagar.

The 18th century Kashmiri romantic poet Arnimal was

a path-breaker. She was born in the conservative Kashmiri Pandit society. She was the daughter of a respectable family and was also wedded to a man from another great family. Her husband was a renowned poet, Munshi Bhagwan Das Kachroo, a Court Poet of Jumma Khan, the Afghan Governor. His poetry flourished during the Afghan period. However, Bhagwan Das was a philanderer, steeped in the dazzling world of the court and the courtesans and was not interested in his wife.

Thus, she lived a loveless life, forsaken by her husband. Not wanting to be cast off as a silent suffering wife, she sang her woes and exposed her husband's infidelity. She was a woman spurned and her poetry told tales of her dejection. For her, speaking of her marital woes became an act of defiance and self-assertion. Arnimal was pretty, imaginative and accomplished but all through her life, she suffered pangs and torments of separation from her husband. She was denied the pleasure of singing, dancing and other creative arts of self-expression but even in such pitiable conditions, she preserved her right to free expression. For Arnimal to speak about the violence and abuse while embedded in a culture of silence was an admirable and courageous act. Her words of brokenheartedness ring loud, reminding us of the suffering women often endure behind closed doors. The domestic unhappiness and the separation from her loved one proved painful and tormenting for Arnimal and her emotions were terribly stirred. After separation from her husband, the spinning wheel became her constant companion and she composed her songs in tune with the sound of the revolving wheel. Its sound could not but remind her of the tragic story of her own life.

As a result of this sorrow and unhappiness was born the most melodious poetry full of pathos and grief as can be seen in the following verses:

1. *Arni Rang Goam Shraavan Yiyey Kar Yiye Darshun Diyey*

The pallor of fading flower has fallen on the midsummer

Jasmine bloom in me. O when shall these eyes see him again?

*Me Kar Tuss Kitch Poshan Maala Ta Aaluv Diya Tosii*

I have made flower garlands for him, Just Hail him, friends.

2. *Tee Kuss Nisha Hykaa Haavith Ba*

That longing, how can I show it to any person?

Arnimal deserves praise and admiration for her boldness in facing misfortunes and for the invaluable contribution which she made to Kashmiri literature through her ordeal and courage. The pictures of delicate sentiments drawn by her in her verses are so vivid, real and charming that very few Kashmiri poets have reached the standard set by her. Most of these lyrics have been set to music and are sung even now by Kashmiris with great interest and gusto.

*April 2019*

While the poetry of Arnimal is devoid of the mystic touch and religious experiences, it speaks of the heart of the human soul.

The lyrics of Arnimal traverse the entire range of emotions, including protests, love, sorrow and weariness like the odes of John Keats. Both of them succeed in transferring their trials and tribulations into universal ones.

Arnimal has become one of the leading lights for the Kashmiri Pandit women who are the best examples of self-sacrifice and embodiments of love. A study of her life and lyrics is enough to establish her poetic genius and mastery of technique achieved despite being unlettered. While belonging to the dark and unhappy age of Afghan rule in Kashmir in the 18th century, she shines as a beacon of light for both Kashmiri men and women.

Arnimal is a great inspiration of resolve, determination and passion for our younger generation of Kashmiri Pandits. She is also a reminder of the values of our great Kashyap Vaer, its creative environment and rich spiritual soil that has produced such great gems.

*Excerpts from Arnimal-A Leading Light by Shri Jai Kishori Pandit and Neerja Mattoo.*

□

# Verses or Vaks of Women Saints of Kashmir

Kashmir, my native land has had a great tradition of women saint poets just like Avvayar and Andal in South and Meera in North India. The most important among them is LalDed or Lalleshwari, a fourteen-century spiritual master, who was the first person to write the spiritual thoughts in the Kashmiri language instead of Sanskrit which was prevalent till then. She was followed by Rupa Bhavani and Riche Ded. All of them were influenced by Kashmir Shaivism. What follows below are some examples of spiritual precepts given by them in the form of their *Vaks*.

**Lal Ded**

1. Oh fool, right action does not lie
   In fasting and other ceremonial rites
2. The temple is but stone
   From top to bottom all is stone
   The pilgrim Sannyasin goes from shrine to shrine
3. Whatever work I did became the worship of Lord
   Whatever word I uttered became a prayer
   Whatever this body of mine experienced
   Became the *sadhana of Shiva Tantra*
   Illuminating my path to *Paramshiva*
4. Some leave their home, some the hermitage

But the restless mind knows no rest
Just watch your breath day and night
And stay where you are.

5. The pilgrim sannyasin goes from shrine to shrine
Seeking to meet Him who abides within himself.
Knowing the truth, O soul, be not misled:
It is the distance that makes the turf look greener.
6. Alike for me is life and death
Happy to live, happy to die
I mourn for none, none mourns for me.

*"atshyan+ aay ta gatushun gatshe*
*Pakun gatshe then kyho raath*
*Yor aya turiy gatshun gatshe*
*Khenata khenata kheneta kyha"*

Forever we come, forever we go;
Forever, day and night, we are on the move.
Whence we come, thither we go,
Forever in the round of birth and death,
From nothingness to nothingness.
But sure, a mystery here abides,
A Something is there for us to know.

## Rupa Bhavani

1. Selflessness is the sign of the selfless
Bow down at the door of the selfless.
The selfless are of the highest authority
The kings of the time and
The wearers of the crest and crown
2. I dashed into the nether regions
And brought the vital breath up.
I got its clue out of earth and stones
Then my *kundalini* woke up with nada;
I drank wine by the mouth and
I got the vital breath gathered within myself

3. I did not come to earth as a seed
   To fall in the circles of births.
   I am not the elements,
   Earth, water, fire, air and ether.
   I am beyond the primordial universal self
   And the individual self
   I am the Supreme Consciousness

## Riche Ded

1. Remembering God, enshrining Him in the heart,
   And reciting His name is the unaffected rosary:
   A guru is necessary for gaining spiritual bliss,
   Which is immortal, imperishable and timeless
2. A kind heart is like a delightful garden,
   Water it fully, and keep it duly fenced:
   A good thought is like a beautiful seed,
   Sow it and, surely raise a bumper crop:
   A sweet word is like a charming flower,
   It disarms enemies and ensures success:
   Benevolence is like a delectable fruit,
   Large-sized and very delicious indeed.

□

# Part-9

# Exodus Stories

# Seven Exoduses: You can Finish me but You can't Finish my Existence

If Hitler is born again and given a chance to re-live his deeds, I am sure he would take tutorials from the last 700 years of Kashmir history and its tyrant rulers who adopted the most inhuman methods to create atrocities, murders and cruelties over the Kashmiri Pandits. His gas chambers will look so feeble and lifeless in front of the systematic inhuman ecosystem that was created not only to murder Kashmiri Pandits and their 5000-year-old culture and heritage but also to convert *Kashyapver*, a land of Saraswat Brahmins to a land of cruel murderers.

We have tried to condense the saga of seven centuries into few pages because we want our young generation to understand the traumatic experience of their forefathers. We also want them to value the courage and valour with which they bounced back each time with tenacity.

## 1st Exodus 1339-1359

After killing Prime Minister Bhatta Bhikshana by deceit and defeating Queen Kota Rani, the last Hindu ruler, Shah Mir took over the throne of Kashmir and established the Shah Miri Dynasty. The Islamisation of Kashmir which began with Rinchen gained force during the rule of the Shah Miri Dynasty.

The most strenuous efforts to convert Hindus to Islam were made during the reign of the sixth Sultan, Sikandar. According to Francis Gautier, the massacres perpetrated by Muslims in India are unparalleled in history, bigger than the holocaust of Jews or massacre of Armenians by the Turks.

It was during his reign that a wave of 700 Sufi warriors, headed by Mir Muhammad Hamadani, arrived in Kashmir to spread Islam aggressively. Sikandar is the most hated figure among the Kashmiri Pandits for committing countless atrocities against non-Muslims and is known as the butcher of Kashmir. He is also called Sikandar Butshikan–Sikandar, the Iconoclast–the idol breaker. This sobriquet was given to him by Muslim historians and not by Hindus.

The Baharistan-i-Shahi says:

To eradicate the traces of Kashmiri Pandits, the rulers institutionalised policies of extermination and subjected them to atrocities and cruelties. The *Jizya* tax of four *tolas* of silver equalling fifty grams was levied on them. They were forced to be converted or killed. "Towards the fag end of his life, Sultan was infused with a zeal for demolishing idol-houses, destroying the temples and the idols. He destroyed the massive temple at Bijbehara (Vijay Vihar) and had designs to destroy all the temples and put an end to the entire community of infidels"

Some were lured to conversion in turn for the royal favours. This created a new class of zealots. Suha Bhatt who after his conversion changed his name to Saif-ud-Din became the leader of neo-converts. It was part of his directives to get all Hindu scriptures collected and thrown into Dal Lake.

He prohibited anyone from wearing a *tilak* on his forehead. All the idols in temples were plundered. The gold and silver idols were melted to make coins.

The Persian biography of Shamsu'd-Din Araki says:

The Sultan prohibited Hindu rites, rituals, and festivals and even wearing the clothes in Hindu style. He did not allow them to blow a conch and prohibited Hindus and Buddhists from cremating their dead.

In his sequel to *Rajatarangini,* Jonaraja wrote, "There was no city, no town, no village, no wood where the temples of gods were not broken. When Sureshwari, Varaha and others were broken, the world trembled but not the mind of the wicked king. Sikandar desecrated and destroyed grand Hindu and Buddhist temples, chaityas, viharas, shrines, hermitages and other holy places. He banned dance, drama, music, iconography, and all other aesthetic activities of Hindus and Buddhists and classified them as heretical. He forgot his royal duties and took delight day and night in breaking images. Sikandar drowned many Hindus in Dal Lake."

According to some sources, only eleven families were left in Kashmir.

According to Farishta:

Many Brahmins rather than abandoning their religion or country poisoned themselves; some emigrated from their homes, while a few escaped the evil of banishment by becoming Muslims.

According to historian Ajit Bhattacharjee,

"Sikandar equalled the most bloodthirsty and iconoclastic Muslim rulers anywhere in his zeal to obliterate all traces of Hindu religion and convert its followers on pain of death." The temples were levelled and some of the grandest monuments of old were damaged and disfigured. For one year, a large establishment was maintained for demolition of the grand Martand Temple. When the massive masonry resisted all efforts, fire was applied and the noble building was cruelly defaced.

According to renowned historian A.K. Mazumdar,

"Sikandar burnt the books of the Hindus the same way as fire burns hay. All the scintillating works faced destruction in the same manner that lotus flowers face with the onset of frosty winter. His reign was disgraced by a series of acts, inspired by religious bigotry and iconoclastic zeal for which there is hardly any parallel in the annals of Muslim rulers of Kashmir.

A Muslim chronicler Hassan records:

"Sikandarpora, a city was founded on the debris of the destroyed temples of the Hindus. In the neighbourhood of the royal gardens of Sikandarpora, Sultan destroyed the temples of Goddesses Kalishree and Maha Shri, one built by King Pravarasena and the other built by Tarapida. The material from these was used for building the Jami Masjid in the middle of the city.

## Imposing the Islamic Law

He decreed that Islamic law be followed instead of the traditional law of Kashmir and created the office of Sheikh-ul-Islam. He issued orders proscribing the residence of any other religion than the Muslims in Kashmir.

This was the first recorded exodus of the indigenous Kashmiri population. The people were given three options, 'conversion, exile or death'. In the Kashmiri language, it is still remembered as *Raliv, Chaliv ya Galiv.* All three options remained in vogue during the entire Muslim rule of 500 years.

There was a major shift in population and the Kashmir valley became predominantly a Muslim majority region. Over the centuries, many Brahmins who did not wish to convert migrated to other parts of the country to escape cruelty. They established themselves in North India, in the courts of Rajputs, Mughals, Nawab's of Awadh, and later, in the courts of Sikhs and Dogras. This cohesive community, highly intelligent, literate and socially elite were one of the first to discuss and promote social reforms in India.

## 2nd Exodus-1413-1430

Sikandar's son, Ali Shah ruled for six years and continued his father's legacy of killings, murders, conversions and *Jizya.* His Prime Minister, Saif-ud-Din continued the crimes and atrocities against the Kashmiri Pandits. Jonaraja gives a graphic account of the plight of the illustrious Kashmiri Pandits in the draconian reign of Ali Shah. He says, 'Saif-ud-Din', the convert passed the limit by levying fine, *jizya* tax on twice-born and also posted squads on the roads to check on any fleeing Pandits. A multitude of celebrated Brahmins, eminent scholars, the pride of the community fled from the country through bye-roads as the main roads were closed. The difficult terrains and forests through which they fled and passed, the scanty food, painful illnesses and the torment of hell they faced during their lifetime removed from their minds the fear of hell. Oppressed by various calamities, lack of food, poisonous snakes and fierce heat, many Brahmins perished on the way and thus obtained salvation." This was the second miserable mass exodus of the Kashmiri Pandits. Jonaraja calls it 'Chandh-Dandh'– violent, cruel, brutal and horrible punishment, for the abandoned and vulnerable Saraswat Brahmins of Kashmir.

## 3rd Exodus-1480-1510

Mir Shams-ud-Din Iraqi came to Kashmir twice in 1477 and 1496. He was the founder of the Nurbakhshiya order, a Shia sect in Kashmir. Not contented with peaceful preachings, violent methods were employed for conversion. Iraqi was helped by the most dreaded tyrant-Malik Musa Raina, a convert, in unleashing the region of terror and forcible conversions. It is said that more than 24,000 persons were forcibly converted to the Shia sect of Islam. Iraqi had even issued orders that every day about 1500 to 2000 Brahmins should be brought to his doorsteps, their sacred threads should be removed and Kalima should be administered to them. After which, they were circumcised and made to eat beef. These decrees were ferociously and brutally carried out leading to another forced exodus of the Kashmiri Pandits.

## 4th Exodus-1630-1675

With the accession of Aurangzeb to the throne, the Kashmiri Pandits were once again made vulnerable due to his bigoted fanatic and dogmatic approach. Iftikhar Khan, the Mughal governor of Kashmir during the reign of Aurangzeb, brutally tyrannised the Brahmins and unleashed his pack of hounds leaving the Kashmiri Pandits no alternative but to embrace Islam on pain of death. During his rule of five years of hair raising cruelty and tyranny, Iftikhar Khan drove it home to Pandits that their future in their land of birth was assured only if they embraced Islam, failing which they must quit their homeland forthwith; there was no third option. Muzaffer Khan, Nassar Khan and Ibrahim Khan were other governors of Aurangzeb who ferociously terrorised the Kashmiri Pandits leading to another forcible, disastrous exodus of Brahmins from their land of origin.

## 5th Exodus-1720-1740

During the rule of the later Mughals, Kashmir witnessed the outbreak of the worst kind of religious intolerance. In 1720, Mullah Abdul Nabi, also called Muhat Khan, a non-resident Kashmiri Muslim, who was appointed as Shaikh-ul-Islam started a campaign of persecution of the Pandits. During his rule, he issued many satanic commandments such as Pandits should not: ride a horse, wear shoes, wear a *Jama,* bear arms, visit any garden, have *tilak* on their forehead, and their children should not receive education. The Pandits were wickedly tormented, their houses burnt and property looted. Hundreds of Brahmins were killed, maimed and humiliated. They began to run away in large numbers and hid in mountainous terrains. This was the fifth dreadful mass exodus of the legendary Kashmiri Pandits from their mystic motherland. Those who remained behind lived in the most horrific and terrible conditions generated by the Mullah and his gang.

## 6th Exodus- 1753-1819

The infamous Afghan rule has been a period of cruelty, homicide and anarchy. W.R. Lawrence calls it the "reign of brutal tyranny." The barbarous Afghans employed every wild, inhuman, primitive, ferocious, cruel and brutal method to suppress the Kashmiri Brahmins. We have heard from our father that Pandits were asked to keep big and deep pockets on both sides of their *pheran* so that any Muslim could jump on the back of a Pandit, put his feet inside the side pockets and take a ride. It is also mentioned that the parents destroyed the beauty of their daughters by shaving their heads or cutting their noses and ears to save them from degradation. The victimised Pandits were forced to flee the country or were killed or converted to Islam. There was a horrible mass exodus of the Kashmiri Pandits to far away places. Many covered long distances on foot.

## 7th Exodus-1930-1949

During the rule of the Sikhs, Dogras and the British, Pandits enjoyed comprehensive religious freedom and social emancipation and political rights. The vicious communal forces turned their wrath against them. During the communal disturbances of July 1931, shops and houses belonging to the Kashmiri Pandits were not only looted but also burnt. This communalism in state politics aggravated and magnified with the passage of time. It was fed for years with vicious communal propaganda and brainwashing and after the independence and accession of Jammu & Kashmir state to India, Kashmiri Pandits were pushed back to the barbarous Afghan era.

They were given sugar-coated doses of poisonous toxins. Article 370 of the Indian constitution just reduced them to cypher and liquidated their population. Under the pretext of economic reforms, their farmlands were confiscated and distributed among the Muslim peasants. The administration of Sheikh Abdullah adopted a malicious and pernicious approach towards the Saraswat Brahmins of Kashmir. They were taunted on one excuse or the other. Hindu temples were desecrated, looted and plundered. Minor girls of the community were forced to change religion and marry the Muslim youth leading to another exodus.

What is important to note is that from the experience of the last seven centuries of horror, tyranny, cruelty, barbarism that the Kashmiri Pandits have gone through, they have also learnt to be fearless and courageous. The entire experience has added to their overall strengths as well. It does not matter how many times we fail but what matters is how many times we get up and bounce back. History is witness that each time we have been hounded, we have learnt new ways of coping. We resurged back time and again. We, the Kashmiri Pandits, will leverage our collective strength to defeat the evil forces and return to 'Satisar' with our heads held high.

We would like to end by sharing a beautiful couplet of Iqbal which echoes our experience:

*Yunan-o-Misr-o-Roma Sab Mit Gaye Jahan Se, Ab Tak Magar Hai Baki Naam-o-Nishan Hamara, Kuchh Baat Hai Ke Hasti Mit'ti Nahin Hamari, Sadiyon Raha Hai Dushman Daur-e-Zaman Hamara*

Meaning:

The great civilisations of Greece, Egypt and Rome got wiped out from the world but we are still around. Even though for centuries we faced the enemy, there is something within us that does not allow us to be wiped out.

*Inspired by and extracts from Dr. Satish Ganjoo's write up-Wailing Kashmir: Seven Migrations of Kashmiri Pandits.*

*Barishta-i-Shahi, (A Chronicle of Medieval Kashmir translated by K.N. Pandita and published by Gulshan Publishers, Srinagar, 2017).*

*Tohfatu'l-Ahbab-translated by K.N. Pandita under the title A Muslim Missionary in Medieval Kashmir.*

□

# Trails of Genocide–Future Implications

Trails of Genocide – Future Implications

People have different perceptions about Kashmir that are far from the reality. Many people continue to believe that

- Kashmir is a Muslim-majority area where Hindus have been a minority.
- Kashmiri Hindus were forced to flee from Kashmir in the year 1990 only.
- Kashmir became an integral part of India only in 1948.
- The glimpse of genocide shown in the movie 'Kashmir Files' is the whole truth.

It is important for people to do a fact-check before arriving at any conclusion. Kashmir has been, for millennia, a cradle of Indian civilisation where many thoughts, beliefs and practices were nurtured. It was once the centre of education which spread the message of unity of all religions to constitute Bharat. Kashmir has produced great scholars like Charaka, Panini, Kalidas, besides Bilhana, Kalhana and Lalitaditya. Lalitaditya's empire spread from the Kaveri basin in south to the Caspian Sea in the north. It was Adi Shankaracharya as also Swami Vivekananda who talked of spiritualism in Kashmir.

Unfortunately, around 13th century when Kashmiris gave refuge to some Muslim Sufis that the situation changed. The pen was crushed with the might of the sword and annihilation of the local Kashmiri Hindus became the order of the day. The ruthless, reckless and relentless killings of Kashmiri Hindus led to a situation where the land belonging to the Hindus in Kashmir was gradually converted to a Muslim land. It is said that thousands of innocent Kashmiri Hindus were murdered in Kashmir and the symbol of their genocide in Kashmir continues to shame the world at a place near Srinagar. This place is called 'Batta Mazar'- the graveyard of Kashmiri Hindus. This genocide continued and it resulted in forced exodus of Hindus almost seven times since then.

Since 1931 onwards, the Kashmiri Hindus were subjected to a very different kind of genocide that eventually led to ethnic cleansing in Kashmir. The genocide as we all know has the intent to destroy partially or fully any minority community. The Kashmiri Hindu community has been victim of this intent again in the last 100 years. The physical genocide which is the core objective in which an ethnic minority community is completely or partially destroyed has been achieved through other means, including political genocide, economic genocide and cultural genocide. Every effort by the establishment had been made to decimate and deprive the minority community of their political, economic and cultural rights. The reorganisation of the electoral constituencies with the intent to render Kashmiri Hindus politically irrelevant has been a part of a larger conspiracy unleashed by the establishment immediately after accession of Jammu and Kashmir into India.

There was never any genuine attempt to reconstruct the temples that were destroyed in Kashmir. In 1972, the introduction of the Land to the Tillers Act by Chief Minister Sheikh Mohammad Abdullah was a major attempt to economically annihilate the Kashmiri Hindus. All this was a part of the larger conspiracy to convert Kashmir, which once a Hindu-majority region, into a Muslim-majority state. It is no surprise that since the last 100 years, there has been a gradual exodus of the minority Kashmiri Hindus on being mentally and physically tortured and forced to leave the Valley. On 19 January 1990, the final nail in the coffin was struck when the majority community came on the roads and loudspeakers blared that the Kashmiri Hindus must leave Kashmir. Subsequently selective killing of Kashmiri Hindus was unleashed wherein thousands of innocent were butchered, leading to a forced exodus of five lakh Kashmiri Hindus from the Kashmir Valley.

The irony of this situation was that since then, the nation, the government in power and the society in large has been in the denial mode about this genocide because it ran counter to the narrative of a particular group in government who subscribed to the policy of appeasement. The height of appeasement and discrimination could be seen through various forms of denial – the denial of genocide, the denial of Justice, the denial of a dignified life in exile, the denial of rehabilitation and return. To live in denial is to live in a vicious cycle of injustice. In the last 32 years, not a single killer has been brought to book and the Hindu community in exile has been forced to live in refugee camps that are more like decorative slums with no basic amenities of quality health, quality education or basic infrastructure. Since then there has only been talk of rehabilitation and return but with no concrete policy or plan for return of nearly 5 lakh Kashmiri Hindus.

With every passing day, the Kashmiri Hindu community in exile has risked a huge cultural disintegration. The movie 'Kashmir Files' is just the tip of the iceberg; a microcosm of the total tragedy that Kashmiri Hindus have gone through. It is therefore important for the establishment to engage with this community, build their morale, confidence and earn their trust and take the following steps that can help resolve this ongoing crisis that this community is going through.

- Accept the genocide.
- Set up a Truth Commission.
- Punish the perpetrators of crime.
- Prepare a plan of action for return and rehabilitation of the sufferers.
- Treat them as internally displaced.

□

# Selfless Shri Bhat and his Seven Demands that brought Light to the Dark Lives of Kashmiri Pandits

The misfortunes, tyranny, killings, murder, cruelty, forcible conversions, annihilation that started from the 14th century resulted in 7 exoduses of Hindus from Kashmir that finally rendered it a Hinduless state.

Only a few Hindu families could live in Kashmir after paying heavy taxes and after tolerating many difficulties and ignominies. The embers of the burnt libraries were still hot. The cries of the raped Hindu women were reverberating in Kashmir. The silence of the ruins of the temples was generating terror. The water of the Vitasta was still red with the blood of the Kashmiri Pandits. Amid this deep darkness, there was still a refulgence from a lamp. While each time the Kashmiri Pandits have bounced back with great tenacity and each time divinity has played by sending its avatars and messiahs, we must be aware of these selfless leaders who have played a key role during these 600 years, in rekindling a ray of hope and making us feel proud of their role and work. One name amongst all is Pandit Shri Bhat, the famous physician of Kashmir.

It was during the reign of Sultan Zain-ul-Abidin, Sikandar's second son that change took place. For some time, Zain-ul-Abidin followed his father's policies of victimisation of

Pandits but later had a change of heart and turned Kashmir once again towards its ancient glory. Many Muslim scholars have attributed it to him saying that Sultan was keen that the land of Sharada should once again shine forth as the fountain of knowledge and learning. Zain-ul-Abidin patronised Sanskrit scholars like Jonaraja, Srivara, Soma Pandit, and Bodhi Bhatt. It was this favourite, devout and learned Kashmiri Pandit physician, Shri Bhat, who converted the Sultan, belonging to the family of heartless and cruel rulers to a nationalist and a secular king.

As a result of the efforts of Sultan Zain-ul-Abidin and Pandit Shri Bhat, the ancient glory of Kashmir started returning. Temples started getting rebuilt, ban was imposed on the slaughter of cows, taxes on Hindus were abolished and the Hindus who had migrated outside Kashmir were invited to return to their homes and given suitable jobs in the government and court.

## The Story behind the Change of Heart of Sultan

Zain-ul-Abidin had hardly completed two years on the throne when a dangerous tumour developed on his chest. Many Syed Hakims treated him but it was of no avail. Well-known Hakims from Central Asia came to treat him but there was no improvement. Sultan then heard that there were Hindu Ayurveda physicians in Kashmir who had the expertise in treating a chronic tumour by incising it. Under the orders of the Sultan, a search for such a doctor was launched but thanks to the activities of the Syeds, Kashmir was bereft of these doctors.

Historian Jonaraja has written that no expert doctor was available because of the repression of Pandits. Ultimately, government officials located Shri Bhat, an expert in treating such tumours. Out of fear, he was reluctant to come and meet the Sultan and kept delaying his arrival in the palace. When he reached the palace, the king encouraged him with his kindness and Shri Bhat started his treatment. While treating the Sultan, Shri Bhat harboured fears of punishment in case the Sultan

did not become well. He was well-versed in treatment but he had started the treatment of Sultan carefully and hesitatingly like the one who touches a diamond shining like fire with hesitation, out of fear of already having suffered burns.

When the Sultan was fully well, he wanted to reward Shri Bhat with jewels and diamonds but Shri Bhat refused to accept any such regard. He did not bother about his comforts and amenities. This attitude of Shri Bhat was something new for the Sultan. He rejected wealth and prosperity and instead, on request of the Sultan, he submitted seven requests which Zain-ul-Abidin gladly accepted. These demands were:

1. The massacre of Hindus based on reasonless religious conflict be stopped immediately and no one is punished without proper investigations and enquiry.
2. Those temples, which were damaged during the time of Sultan Sikandar, be rebuilt. Permission is given to those Hindus, who had been forcibly converted to Islam, to return to the religion of their ancestors. Those Kashmiris who had migrated out of fear to areas outside Kashmir, where they were leading a life of penury, be immediately invited back to their houses.
3. The Sanskrit schools be reopened and facilities be made available there for the study of scriptures by the Hindu students for their development and progress.
4. The taxes imposed on the Hindus be abolished and they be given equal rights.
5. While respecting the religious sentiments of the Hindus, cow slaughter be banned.

6. The ban on performing *Yagnya* and rites and customs of Hindus be lifted.
7. Immediate repair of libraries, set ablaze by the Sultans, be undertaken.

The Sultan accepted all the requests submitted by Shri Bhat and Hindus once again enjoyed secular governance under Sultan Zain-ul-Abidin.

The famous historian, Abul Fazal, has, while giving an introduction of Shri Bhat in his biography of Akbar titled 'Aain-e-Akbari', writes that Zain-ul-Abidin would have also followed the tainted tide which was carried out by his father and brother but for the efforts of Shri Bhat. It is because of the efforts of Shri Bhat that Pandit families returned to Kashmir for resettlement. Under his guidance, the government appointed them on different posts in the government as per their calibre. Shri Bhat successfully resolved all the problems connected with their resettlement, their family arrangements, their security and their identity while linking them with the then administrative setup.

*Reference and excerpts from Converted Kashmir: Memorial of Mistakes by Narender Sehgal.*

□

# Martyrdom of Guru Tegh Bahadur

In 1587, Akbar deceptively acquired Kashmir from the Chaks and banished the ruler Yusuf Shah Chak to Bihar. In Kashmir, Akbar continued his policies of religious tolerance. A large number of Hindus still existed in Kashmir during his reign. However, the situation worsened after him especially during the rule of Aurangzeb, who once again launched a reign of terror against Kashmiri Pandits. At this dark moment, Kashmiri Pandits turned to Guru Tegh Bahadur Sahib, the 9$^{th}$ Guru in the lineage of Guru Nanak for guidance and help.

## Guru Tegh Bahadur

There is a legend recorded by Bhai Gyan Singh Gyani and Bhai Santosh Singh Gyani during the reign of Maharaja Ranjeet Singh. It tells the tale of 500 Kashmiri Brahmins arriving in Anandpur Sahib to seek help from Guru Tegh Bahadur. They had first gone to Amarnath to obtain guidance from Lord Shiva. It is said that at Amarnath, the leader of the contingent had a dream in which Lord Shiva appeared and directed them to seek help from Guru Tegh Bahadur.

After listening to the pitiable tale of Kashmiri Pandits and the atrocities unleashed on them, Guru Tegh Bahadur went from Anandpur Sahib to Delhi to meet the Mughal Emperor Aurangzeb, to request him to stop the forced conversion and massacre of Kashmiri Pandits. In the process, Guru Tegh Bahadur sacrificed his own life and was beheaded by cruel, bigoted Aurangzeb.

## Gurudwara Sisganj

At Gurudwara Sisganj in Chandni Chowk in Old Delhi, the marble platform under the long window is the location where Guru Tegh Bahadur was beheaded publicly by Aurangzeb on 11th November, 1675.

His son, Guru Gobind Singh, in his composition titled, Bachittar Natak has given an account of his father's sacrifice. It says that the Guru had promised to protect Kashmiri Hindus and resisted their persecution. He was summoned to Delhi by Aurangzeb on the pretext of a meeting. However, when he arrived, he was arrested and asked to convert to Islam. The Bachitar Natak is recited in every Sikh temple on the occasion of the Guru Tegh Bahadur's martyrdom.

According to William Irvine:

Guru Tegh Bahadur was tortured for many weeks while being asked to abandon his faith and convert to Islam; he stood by his convictions and refused; he was then publicly executed.

The Guru's associates were also tortured for refusing to convert. Bhai Mati Das was sawn into pieces, Bhai Sati Das was executed wrapped in cotton wool soaked in fuel and set to fire and Bhai Dayala was tied with an iron chain and made to stand erect into a big cauldron of water filled up to his neck. It was set on fire and he was boiled to death. While all this was going on, Guru Tegh Bahadur was held inside a cage to watch his colleagues suffer. The Guru himself was beheaded in the middle of Chandni Chowk. The head and the body of the Guru were whisked away by his disciples before the emperor's guards could lay their dirty hands on them.

## Gurudwara Rakab Ganj Sahib and other Gurudwaras

Apart from Gurudwara Sisganj, many other Sikh temples were built in memory of Guru Tegh Bahadur. Gurudwara Rakab Ganj Sahib in Delhi was built on the site of the residence of a disciple of Guru Tegh Bahadur,who burned his entire house to secretly cremate his master's body without the knowledge of Aurangzeb.

Gurudwara Sisganj Sahib in Punjab marks the site where the head of Guru Tegh Bahadur was brought by Bhai Jaita and cremated in defiance of Aurangzeb. Guru Tegh Bahadur is remembered for sacrificing his life for the freedom of religion, reminding Sikhs and non-Muslims in India to follow and practice their faith without fear of persecution and resisting the forced conversions by Muslims.

## Effect on the Formation of Sikh Identity

The execution of Guru hardened the resolve of Sikhs against Muslim rule. Eminent Sikh Scholar, Pashaura Singh states:

If the martyrdom of the Guru Arjan had helped to bring the Sikh Panth together, Guru Tegh Bahadur's martyrdom helped to make the protection of human rights central to the Sikh identity.

Wilfred Smith mentions:

"The attempt to forcibly convert the Ninth Guru to an externalised, impersonal Islam made an indelible impression on the martyr's nine year-old son, Gobind, who reacted slowly but deliberately by eventually organising the Sikh group into a distinct, formal, symbol-patterned community. It inaugurated the Khalsa identity."

We were fortunate to have visited Anandpur Sahib and blessed by entering the house of Guru Tegh Bahadur Sahib as well as partake of langar at Gurudwara Anandpur Sahib. At this holy spot, we also learnt the Sikh version of the Ninth Guru's martyrdom which was narrated to us as follows:

"After suffering from Aurangzeb's killing spree, a delegation of 500 Kashmiri pandits who were divinely guided to meet the Guru reached Anandapur Sahib. They petitioned Guru about their pathetic situation. To them, at that time, he was the highest spiritual authority in India,who could guide them.

The Guru's nine-year son, Gobind, was also present during this meeting. After the delegation left, Gobind asked his father what was to be done to stop this massacre. The Guru replied, "It can only be stopped if a great man sacrifices his life." The son seems to have replied, "Father who could be a greater man than you in India to challenge Aurangzeb." Hearing this, the father resolved to leave for Delhi and meet Aurangzeb without further delay. Later, the little boy became the founder of Khalsa Panth and came to be known as the Tenth Sikh Guru, Guru Gobind Singh.

## Three Hundredth Year of Khalsa

The Three hundredth year of Khalsa was celebrated in India in the year 2007. One of the high points of the celebrations was arranged by Kashmiri Pandits to commemorate the sacrifice of the Ninth Guru. A *Jatha* of 300 Kashmiri Pandits, including some of our friends visited Sisganj Sahib to pay homage to Guru Tegh Bhadur. We, Kashmiri Pandits must realise that we owe our existence to the sacrifice of the Ninth Guru. Our parents deeply respected gurus and our mothers did Karseva for langar in Gurudwaras and we were brought up listening to the sacred kirtan.

□

# Bhatta Mazar—
# The Graveyard of Pandits

The story of Kashmir Pandits for many centuries has been an unending nightmare of atrocities by successive Muslim rulers. One glaring example of it is the 'Bhatta Mazar', the graveyard of Brahmins. When we were small children, our fathers told us about the existence of this graveyard. At that time, we never realised the gravity of the tragedy till we learnt more about it and its deep impact on the Kashmiri Pandits as a community. We also wish that our younger generation must know and remember the history.

In 14th century, the radical and bigoted Islam bared all its intolerant fangs under the sixth ruler of the Shah Miri Dynasty, Sultan Sikandar who was honoured with the title of Butshikan, the iconoclast, the idol breaker, by the Muslim historians. He bulldozed almost all grand Hindu temples in the state. He ordered the bodies of the slain Hindus to be thrown into the Dal Lake but not before cutting their sacred threads off their bodies and burning them. This yielded him a grand harvest of seven maunds-equal to 261 kilograms of the sacred thread. This torture, brutality and killings continued for many more centuries.

According to Lawrence, it was the practice to tie up the Brahmins, two into two, in grass sacks and sink them in the Dal Lake as an amusement. A pitcher filled with ordure would be placed on a Pandit's head and a Muslim would pelt the pitcher with stones till it broke and the unfortunate Pandit got blinded with filth.

Mir Hazar was another fiend who used leather bags instead of grass sacks for the drowning of Pandits. He drowned Pandits indiscriminately. Today, this place of these gruesome crimes is known as Bhatta Mazar, the graveyard of Pandits.

Lawrence again says that,

The kind of torture inflicted on Pandits, and the savage mentality of these rulers was so ferocious that Kashmiri Hindu parents who rather than allowing the degradation of their daughters, destroyed their beauty by shaving their heads or cutting their noses.

Shri M.K. Raina in his 'Afghan Ruler in Kashmir' writes that the barbarity was so deep during the Afghan rule that out of fear of the bridegroom being abducted or killed, the custom of having a *'Pot Maharaza'* proxy or substitute bridegroom was introduced. This young man dressed like the bridegroom accompanied the bridegroom. In case something untoward happened to the bridegroom, the *'Pot Maharaza'* would immediately take his place.

Despite forcible conversions, murders, atrocities and the misfortune of living under the most inhospitable and unsympathetic political and administrative environment, repeatedly over the last seven centuries, the Pandit community has survived and resurged against all odds. This is an unprecedented example of their strength and tenacity.

Despite being reduced to just *'Kah Ghara'*,eleven families, "We are there and we are what we are."

□

# Birbal Dhar—Liberator of Kashmir from Afghan Clutches

Kashmiri Hindus did not lose courage despite being the victims of atrocities for 500 years of the barbaric rule of the foreigners. Yet by the 19th century, it had become tired and exhausted of tolerating and facing atrocities that lasted up to the rule of the last Afghan Subedar. When the Sikh kingdom was established in Punjab, Kashmiri Pandits wished to contact Sikh Maharaja and seek his help to protect the Hindu society in this situation.

A secret meeting was organised for carrying out the sacred duty of protecting their society in the interest of nationalism. Political, religious and social Hindu leaders from the entire state participated in the meeting which was held in the house of Mirza Pandit. After the deliberation, it was decided to approach Maharaja Ranjit Singh for help. The hero of this accomplishment was Pandit Birbal Dhar. He was a leader of the Kashmiri resistance to Afghan Rule and led the deputation which persuaded Maharaja Ranjit Singh to invade Kashmir in 1819 and effectively ended Afghan and Muslim rule in Kashmir. They willingly took up the responsibility of meeting the Maharaja.

In order to meet Maharaja Ranjit Singh, Birbal Pandit left the house along with his son, Raja Kak, in disguise leaving his wife and daughter-in-law behind. After halting at Devsar, they left for their onward journey. They marched towards their destination carefully, surmounting many hurdles in the way. As a result of their strong faith in their objective, they could secure the assistance of many other families on the way and many more Hindus from Kashmir followed them.

They were successful in reaching the court of Maharaja Gulab Singh in Jammu. Maharaja Gulab Singh gave a letter to Raja Dhian Singh, Prime Minister of Maharaja Ranjit Singh, and made arrangements for their trip to Lahore. On reaching Lahore, Raja Dhian Singh organised their meeting with Maharaja Ranjit Singh. Pandit Birbal narrated the entire sad story of the plight of the Hindus to the Maharaja.

Maharaja was highly impressed by the oratory and scholarship of Birbal Dhar. He listened to Birbal attentively. He was dismayed over the misfortune of Hindus and the destruction of Indianness in Kashmir. He felt that the entire problem should be viewed in the national context. He was a true Sikh who recalled the sacrifice of Guru Teg Bahadur. The picture of the young children of Shri Gobind Singh being embedded in the wall loomed large in front of his eyes. He could see the severed head of Guru Teg Bahadur before his eyes.

After discussing the matter with his associates, Maharaja immediately ordered that the troops be kept ready. He suggested to Birbal Dhar to remain with the army officers for acquainting them with the topography of the state and guiding them.

Pandit Birbal accepted all the conditions and kept his son in the Lahore court as a hostage. When Subedar of Kashmir, Azam Khan learnt about the ensuing invasion of Kashmir by the Sikh soldiers, he was scared. He felt he would be asked to give an account of all his evil deeds. He was so terrified that he sent his harem, his entire gold and wealth to Kabul. After a few days, he also left Kashmir and handed over the power to his brother, Jabbar Khan. Even while fleeing Kashmir, Azam Khan committed a condemnable act of kidnapping a wealthy Pandit, Suraj Tikoo for ransom so that he could grab his wealth. Unfortunately, he could not lay hands on his wealth and so he killed Suraj Tikoo near Baramulla.

Maharaja Ranjit Singh sent his five top and brave army commanders along with 30,000 soldiers to Kashmir under the guidance of Pandit Birbal. They were Raja Gulab Singh of Jammu, Hari Singh Nalwa, Jwala Singh, Hukum Singh and Shyam Singh. They uprooted the troops of Jabbar Khan with their might. Jabbar Khan took to his heels and ran away. The Sikh soldiers emerged victorious and brought about an end to Afghan rule.

On 20 June, 1819 A.D., Pandit Birbal along with Sikh soldiers entered Kashmir as a victor. Even Muslim historians have praised the contribution of Pandit Birbal. According to Muhammad Din Fauq, Pandit Birbal was a person of bright character. For achieving this victory, he had to make a great personal sacrifice. In his view, any great sacrifice was much too small for the noble cause before him. When Azam Khan came to know about Birbal's march to Lahore, he ordered the capture of his wife and daughter-in-law. After capture, his wife committed suicide, by jumping into the Vitasta river while his daughter-in-law was caught, converted and taken to Kabul and was never found again.

He remained calm amid the suicide of his loyal wife, abduction and forcible conversion of his daughter-in-law and the merciless killings of his friends and relations. Despite all that, he kept marching with determination on his path so that he could throw out the Afghans from his country.

Even in the hour of his triumph, he did not forget his Muslim countrymen as well and his duty. The historians mention that the Sikh army wanted to loot the city and demolish the sacred shrine of Shah Hamdan which was built after destroying the temple of Goddess Kalishree, but Birbal came in their way to stop the destruction of Shah Hamdan mosque. Without caring for his personal safety, he told Phool Singh, the Sikh Commander that history will condemn him for his evil deeds if he looted the Muslim population of the city or destroyed the mosques.

This noble act of Birbal is sufficient to make him immortal. He is a symbol of the innate qualities of Pandits and of their permanent strength to fight the onslaughts of time. The character of Pandit Birbal reveals that if a single person desires, he can change the course of history. Success is assured if one remains above self-interest and works with dedication and determination during the hour of national crisis. The role played by Pandit Birbal and his son for finishing the cruel rulers of Kashmir has in its background the encouragement of two great women who lost and sacrificed everything for completing the national task.

Due to his role in ending the cruel Afghan rule, Birbal Dhar was made the Talukdar of Kashmir by Maharaja Ranjit Singh. He was also given a place in his council of Ministers which he refused because he wanted to remain close to his people and did not wish to leave Kashmir and go to the court of Lahore.

Had Pandit Birbal desired, he could have sought revenge after his victory. He could have avenged the destruction of temples and educational institutions during the last 500 years from mosques and tombs but as a great man as he was, he did nothing like this.

*Excerpts are taken from Converted Kashmir: Memorial of Mistakes by Narender Sehgal.*

□□□